DO NOT REMOVE
CARDS FROM POCKET

ALLEN COUNTY PUBLIC LIBRARY

FORT WAYNE, INDIANA 46802

You may return this book to any agency, branch,
or bookmobile of the Allen County Public Library.

DEMCO

PRACTICAL GUIDE TO **CATS**

Hamlyn
London · New York
Sydney · Toronto

PRACTICAL GUIDE TO
CATS

Ivor Raleigh PhD · Patricia Scott PhD
Elizabeth Jackson BSc MRCVS
Oliphant Jackson PhD MRCVS

Acknowledgements

Front jacket Sally Anne Thompson; *inset left* Hamlyn Group Picture Library; *inset centre* Animal Graphics Ltd; *inset right* Hamlyn Group Picture Library. *Back jacket* Sally Anne Thompson.

Colour illustrations
Animal Graphics Ltd 22 top, 22 bottom, 23 top, 26 top, 27, 30 top, 30 bottom, 31, 50 top, 50 bottom, 51, 54 top, 55, 59 bottom, 62 top, 66 top, 67 bottom, 71 top, 71 bottom, 74, 75 top, 75 bottom, 79, 98 top, 99, 110 bottom; Bruce Coleman Ltd – S. C. Bisserot 19, Rod Borland 18, Jane Burton 78 bottom, Hans Rheinhard 67 top; Anne Cumbers 78 top; Paul Kaye 58 top, 59 top, 62 bottom, 66 bottom; Keystone Press Agency Ltd 23 bottom; Popperfoto 26 bottom, 54 bottom, 63, 70, 98 bottom, 102, 103 top, 103 bottom, 106 top, 106 bottom, 107, 110 top, 111; Nick Wright 58 bottom.

Black and white illustrations
Animal Graphics Ltd title pages, 17, 40, 41 bottom, 43, 46 top, 47, 53, 57, 64, 77, 92, 95, 96, 105, 108, 109, 121; Anne Cumbers 68; Will Green 46 bottom, 49; Paul Kaye 45, 118; Naturfoto – Elvig Hansen 7, 10, 11, 13, 15 top, 15 bottom, 16, 32 top, 32 bottom, 34 top, 34 bottom, 35, 36, 72–73, Karl Holgard 28; Pictorial Press Ltd 41 top; Popperfoto 20, 37, 39, 69; Royal Free Hospital School of Medicine 113; John Topham Picture Library 33, 83, 91, 123.

The photographs on pages 76, 80 and 89 were reproduced with the kind permission of Cat Accessories Ltd, Bedford.

Line drawings by Jennifer Middleton

The publishers would like to thank the Gaines Dog Research Center for permission to reproduce the chart on page 85, which was based on material taken from the *Gaines Basic Guide to Canine Nutrition*, 3rd edition, 1974.

Published by The Hamlyn Publishing Group Limited
London · New York · Sydney · Toronto
Astronaut House, Feltham, Middlesex, England
Copyright © The Hamlyn Publishing Group Limited 1976

ISBN 0 600 31810 9

Phototypeset by Tradespools Limited, Frome, Somerset
Printed in Great Britain by Hazell Watson & Viney Ltd, Aylesbury, Buckinghamshire

Contents

Introduction

The universal popularity of the domestic cat is beyond dispute and throughout history, its praises have been sung by poets and storytellers in every tongue. Some of this praise has been engendered by the cat's usefulness as a destroyer of vermin, but no doubt the principal roots of the cat's success lie in its grace together with its impact upon one of man's own psychological needs.

The concept of beauty is astonishingly constant throughout the human race, and such regional and individual variations as do exist are comparatively minor and are often the result of limited choice rather than of differences. It is evident that the lithe grace, the superb proportions, the beauty and texture of coat, the general air of charm and the friendly nature, all of which are so well combined in the cat, are qualities which induce an immediate and highly favourable response in most people.

It has been said that the company of a charming and affectionate animal is very meaningful to many people who, perhaps because of shyness, find it difficult to establish a close relationship with their neighbours. For such people an obvious and acceptable alternative would be to lavish their abundant natural affection upon an animal which is beautiful, quiet, discriminating, affectionate, receptive of affection and, above all, one which never blames or criticizes hurtfully. Thus we see that the two main reasons for man's devotion to the cat are its beauty and its compatibility with man. If we also consider that cats are easy and inexpensive to keep, are clean about the house and are good with children, it becomes easy to understand why so many people choose to own one or more of them. By comparison the dog, another delightful animal, perhaps does not complement man so successfully because it slavishly accepts the more unpleasant side of his nature.

Man is a gregarious creature, and from the earliest times it has been his custom to form clubs or societies with others having common interests. Cat lovers of the world have generally followed this time-honoured pattern with the result that all over the world there is a large range of cat clubs which provide focuses for cat fanciers and which organize shows where experienced judges compare the results of breeding against standards of points. These shows also constitute a market place in which cats can be bought and sold, views can be exchanged and advice sought and obtained.

The first large-scale cat society in the world was probably founded in Britain in the late 1800s, and thereafter similar organizations began in the United States of America and on the Continent and were largely founded upon the British pattern. This position has been more or less maintained to the present day, with the British standards of points forming the basis upon which all other standards are constructed. Nevertheless, the American Cat Fancy has given recognition to a few varieties of cat so far unrecognized in Britain. The continental Fancies, on the other hand, have adhered closely to British standards. Similarly, the rules for the exhibition of cats used in Europe and the United States are closely based upon the British pattern with the notable exception that whereas British shows never extend to more than a single day, continental and American shows always last two days.

In an essentially practical book it is not really feasible to discuss at length the subject of how far cats can think. Equally, it would seem to be wrong to leave out altogether at least an elementary survey of the mental capabilities of cats; capabilities upon the existence of which the man–cat relationship is so largely founded.

To understand the processes underlying manifested mental ability we must first look at the dimensional aspect of thought. According to William James, Bucke and Ouspensky all mammals, including man, see objects two-dimensionally. In man alone, a higher faculty exists, whereby although he sees objects in two dimensions, his intellect and his ability to form concepts enable him to add a third dimension. A man

The cat, thinking and seeing two-dimensionally, contemplates the snail and ponders upon its potential edibility, while the snail, seeing and thinking in one dimension, relies upon the pleasure-pain syndrome and its inherent instincts and turns away from an unknown danger.

travelling in a car will see trees and houses rushing towards him and turning round as they move. A cat, a dog or a horse will observe the same effect; but whereas the intellectual and conceptual ability in man will enable him to realize that this motion is merely an illusion, the animal will accept it as true motion. A horse shying at a bush as it runs past does so because the bush appears to have just raised a branch to strike out at it.

Because cats cannot form concepts but rely entirely on percepts, true thought, in the human sense, is not possible to them; and we know that they are incapable of conceptual thought because, had they been capable, it is virtually a certainty that they would have evolved a language. To a cat every man is a unique individual and each house or tree is also an individual. The concept 'man', 'trees', 'houses', is beyond their reach. Their thinking is based upon simple arithmetic whereas man's thinking is based on algebra. For this reason cats and other animals fill their limited brains with a tremendous collection of facts, leaving no room for intellectual growth. It is this, and not the fact that animals have settled for specialization, which limits their advancement for ever.

Living in their two-dimensional world cats are guided by their animal grace, by their instinct and by the pain-pleasure syndrome. To a cat, its owner is the person who feeds it and gives it pleasure; its home

is where it can obtain food and rest and quiet. It returns these gifts by giving what amounts to a love-like response. For a cat to think in the way in which man thinks, it would have to develop the ability to form concepts and to substitute reason for instinct. We know that the cat is not capable of this, although some of its instinctive responses have a superficial resemblance to actual thought, and a man or woman who considers a cat through the eyes of love can easily be persuaded that it is reasoning conceptually. Indeed, it would be wrong to say that on rare occasions it is not just about possible for a cat to transcend its limitations and momentarily to glimpse the three-dimensional, conceptual universe which is commonplace to man. Likewise, man is limited in his understanding of the universe by his inability to see it as a four-dimensional continuum. A few rare individuals have transcended this limitation and have been immediately recognized by their contemporaries as men apart. They were called seers and messiahs and were the founders of the great religions.

If you have read this far you probably have more than a passing interest in cats, and you should now become acquainted with the scope and purpose of this book and how it differs from many other books about cats. Each chapter is packed with information which will fascinate every cat lover, tell you more about cats and their behaviour and how you can enjoy your pet to the full.

Characteristics

THE CAT FAMILY

Cats are members of the mammalian order Carnivora, whose fossilized ancestors have been found as far back as the Eocene period (thirty-five to sixty million years ago). The cat family evolved as predators, obtaining their food by chasing, killing and consuming other animals. Depending on the size of the predator, the prey may be as small as an insect or larger than an antelope. A common habit of alertness and the ability to move swiftly and gracefully has made the carnivores the delight of human beings since prehistory. The Carnivora are characterized by modifications of the fourth upper premolar and the first lower molar teeth to form the *carnassials*; these teeth cut through tough skin and flesh with a scissor-like action, and, aided by the other molars, can crush bones. Canine teeth are also well developed for biting the prey, thereby inflicting fatal wounds in the throat or back of the neck. Enormous canine teeth have been found in fossils of sabre-toothed carnivores but these animals were not well suited for survival in other ways. At an early stage of their evolution the carnivores separated into a group basically dog-like in pattern (the Canoidea) and another which was cat-like (the Feloidea). The modern family Felidae contains the wild cats, ocelot, serval, caracal, lynxes, puma, leopard, jaguar, lion, tiger and cheetah. Small wild cats of the genus *Felis* are found in Europe, Asia and Africa.

The African wild cat *F. libyca* is widely distributed in North Africa, southern Europe and central Asia. Most of the sacred mummified cats of Ancient Egypt (circa 1600 BC) have been found to belong to this species. The European wild cat *F. silvestris* is still found in forests in Europe (including Britain) and south-east Asia but is in danger of extinction owing to the loss of its habitat. The jungle cat *F. chaus* is found in Egypt and south-east Asia. A few of the Egyptian mummies also belonged to this species. The Chinese desert cat *F. bieti* and the sand cat *F. margarita* are desert species, the latter being found around the Sahara, Arabian

and central Asian deserts. The black-footed cat of South Africa is *F. nigripes*. Modern domestic cats throughout the world belong to the species *F. catus*; the most closely related wild species seem to be *F. libyca* and *F. silvestris*, and *F. catus* may have arisen from crossings of these species.

Varieties of domestic cat do not differ greatly in size, the largest being about twice as heavy as the smallest. This is in marked contrast to domestic dogs, the largest varieties of which are about two hundred times the weight of the smallest. An adult male (tom) cat has a broader head and is generally larger boned than the adult female (queen) cat; he should weigh between 7 and 12 pounds (3·0 and 5·5 kg) whereas she should weigh between 5 and 7 pounds (2·25 and 3·0kg).

A reconstruction of a miacid, based on fossil evidence. These prehistoric forebears were excellent hunters and gave rise to several carnivore groups, including the cat family.

THE SKELETON AND ASSOCIATED BODY ORGANS

Cats are lithe animals and their shape is

developed for rapidly pouncing, springing, jumping, climbing and running short distances. To carry out these activities, the skeleton is lightly built on the general mammalian plan.

The head is carried high on seven cervical (neck) vertebrae, the first two being specially modified to allow the cat to turn its head from side to side as well as up and down. The cervical vertebrae are supported by exceptionally strong neck muscles which position the head for searching the surroundings, sighting, catching and carrying the prey. A mother cat can also carry a heavy kitten considerable distances over high obstacles.

The thirteen thoracic (dorsal) vertebrae each articulate with a pair of ribs, the headward seven pairs being joined to the sternum below and the remainder each to the one above to form a capacious cage. This houses the heart, lungs and large blood vessels. The thorax (chest) is closed tailward by a sheet of arched muscle and tendon, the diaphragm. As the muscles used in breathing lift the ribs, the diaphragm contracts and flattens and air is automatically sucked into the lungs through the nasal passages and trachea (windpipe). When a cat is sitting or lying quietly, respiratory movements are so shallow and infrequent (twenty per minute) that one has to watch carefully to see them. But after exercise or when a cat is overheated, frightened, in pain or feverish the frequency and depth of respiration increase greatly. When a cat is very hot it pants, opening its mouth and pushing air in and out rapidly in an attempt to dissipate excess heat by evaporating water from the mucous membranes lining the mouth and respiratory tract. Another use of the thoracic bellows is to pump air across the vocal cords in the throat which, when actively vibrated by the animal, produce calls and cries and the characteristic purr of contentment.

Seven stout lumbar vertebrae form the strong, supple back. Arching and springing movements are made possible by large bundles of muscles running down the back, which are attached to the lumbar as well as to the thoracic and sacral vertebrae. The lumbar vertebrae carry the weight of the suspended abdominal organs – the stomach, intestines, liver, spleen, kidneys and bladder. In the female the ovaries and uterus are also suspended and become very

A skeleton of the cat showing the position of the principal bones. The limbs are adapted for running, jumping and climbing.

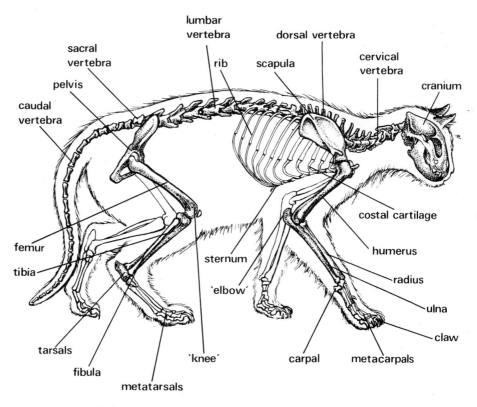

heavy in pregnancy. The smooth sheets of tissue which act as slings and carry the supplying arteries, veins and nerves to the intestines and two horns of the uterus, allow movement and distension of the tubes to occur. The stomach and bladder are also variably distensible. The peritoneal (abdominal) cavity is closed below by a muscular, fibrous wall, which again permits variable distension of the viscera. A 'droopy middle' is the result either of a fracture or of softening of the lumbar vertebrae, which is sometimes due to calcium deficiency in kittenhood but more commonly to loss of tone in the abdominal muscles due to excessive fat or heavy kittening. The arched diaphragm allows the soft, vulnerable liver, spleen and stomach to be tucked underneath the ribs. The kidneys are protected by fat and firmly bound to the roof of the abdominal cavity under the most posterior ribs. The bladder, when full, can be felt in the lower part of the abdomen; it is connected to the kidneys by the ureters and to the exterior by a tube called the urethra.

In the male the ducts leading from the testes open into the urethra, which acts as a common passage for urine and semen which exit via the penis. In the female the urethra is separate from the vagina (birth canal) which connects the uterus with the exterior. In both sexes the anus has a separate opening just under the tail.

Three fused sacral vertebrae make a firm, immovable joint with the pelvic girdle. Twenty or so vertebrae attached to the sacrum form the support for the long, supple tail, the bones gradually reducing in size and complexity towards the tip. They are joined by tendons and small muscles, the only powerful muscles being at the root attached to the sacrum and pelvis. The cat uses its tail for balancing, especially when springing, but cannot grip a branch to aid in climbing. The tail is an important signalling organ, actively expressing the emotional state of the animal. Manx cats have an heritable defect in which all but three or four of the tail bones fail to develop.

The cat walks and runs by digitigrade

Below and right **Strong neck muscles enable the mother cat to carry her kitten in her mouth, while extension of the leg muscles gives force to the spring carrying her up to the chosen retreat. Note the balancing tail.**

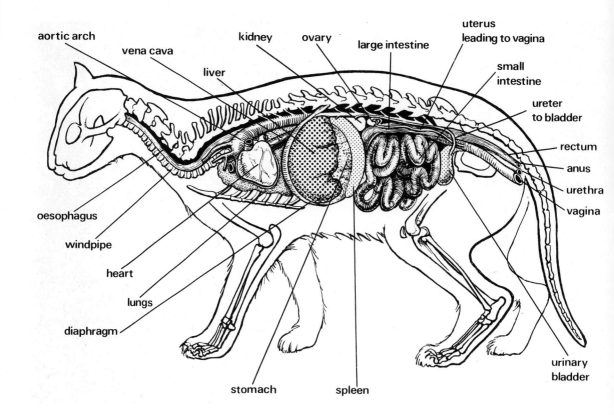

aortic arch
vena cava
liver
kidney
ovary
large intestine
uterus leading to vagina
small intestine
ureter to bladder
rectum
anus
urethra
vagina
oesophagus
windpipe
heart
lungs
diaphragm
stomach
spleen
urinary bladder

progression; that is, the long, slender limbs are balanced on pads under the digits (fingers and toes) forming a paw. The digits, five in front and four behind, end in highly specialized claws which are normally sheathed but, by the action of the muscle and tendon shown in the illustration, can be protracted to catch and hold prey, in climbing, in fighting or in attempting to escape. The forepaw can be rotated because the radius can travel round the ulna while the wrist bones are fixed. Since the head of the humerus is held in a shallow depression on the scapula, which also moves freely held only by muscles on to the chest wall, the whole forearm becomes an incredibly adaptable structure. The forelimb can be moved across the chest for washing, climbing and holding, and backwards and forwards in running. The forepaw is able to grasp objects and scoop them up but the cat cannot oppose the first digit (thumb) to the others because the long, slender metacarpals are tightly bound together to enable the cat to run. Thus cats are unable to handle tools in the way that monkeys and apes are able to do. The hindlimb, more rigidly fixed, moves in only one plane, for-

wards and backwards. The light but strong pelvic girdle forms a deep cup for the articulation of the femur and is firmly bound to the sacral vertebrae. Muscular

Above **Diagrammatic representation of the arrangement of the principal internal organs in an entire female cat.**

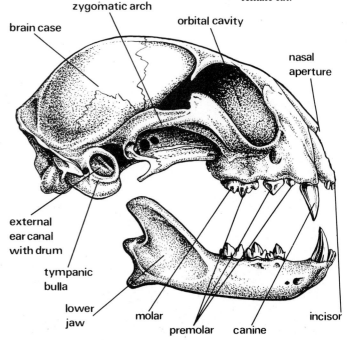

brain case
zygomatic arch
orbital cavity
nasal aperture
external ear canal with drum
tympanic bulla
lower jaw
molar
premolar
canine
incisor

development in this region is tremendous and the knee (bent in the opposite direction to the elbow), combines with the ankle joint in a spring-like mechanism thrusting the body forward in running and jumping. The hindpaws are adapted for obtaining a firm push-off from the ground and also take part in climbing. At the same time, when the joints are acutely flexed and the muscles are relaxed, the cat is able to sit comfortably.

THE HEAD
Skull, jaws and teeth

The head is the most characteristic feature of cats. Broad and short nosed, it is carried high and forward so that the mouth, eyes and ears are most advantageously placed for detecting and capturing the prey. The skull consists of a large, rounded brain case, regions specialized for the ears, eyes and nose, and a strong pair of jaws. The maxillae (upper jaws) are firmly attached, but the mandibles (lower jaws) are hinged so that the mouth can be opened wide for biting, or slide sideways for mastication. The jaws carry thirty permanent teeth which are preceded by a milk dentition cut soon after birth. The incisors are small and often lost in older cats without detriment, but a broken canine or decayed carnassial may prevent the cat from eating and thus result in death in the wild state. The canines are used to catch and kill the prey by a clean

bite through the back of the neck between the vertebrae. These teeth, and the gums surrounding them, are supplied with exceptionally numerous, large, sensory nerves which are thought to make it possible for the cat to select exactly the right place for biting. Bones and other 'hard tack' should be provided to keep the teeth exercised, except in very young or very old cats. The lower jaws are powered by exceptionally strong muscles of mastication attached to the skull which, with the well-developed zygomatic arch, give the characteristic width to the face.

Eyes

Cat's eyes are large, protruding and set in deep sockets in the skull. The eyes cannot move freely, however, and the cat has to turn its head – and often its body – towards a point of interest in order to bring an object into focus on the central part of the retina where daylight vision is clearest. Experiments have shown that while cats can be trained, with difficulty, to discriminate between colours, they do not ordinarily use colour vision in recognizing objects. Human beings have better daylight vision but cats come into their own at night for they are able to see in the dimmest of lights, that is, in conditions of apparent total darkness to the human eye. The iris becomes relaxed and the pupil widely dilated. Light passes through the curved cornea and lens and on to the retina, and is reflected back again by a special layer, the tapetum. The effect of this layer can be seen, shining yellow, when a cat stares at the headlights of a car in the dark. It is possible that the tapetum or retina itself has a photomultiplier effect rather like modern night fieldglasses. This delicate mechanism must be protected from strong, direct sunlight during the day so the cat's iris, which is pigmented (coloured) to prevent light passing through it, contracts with the help of a special muscle to form a vertical slit-like pupil. This controls the amount of light entering the eye more effectively than the round pupil of the human or dog.

Because the eyes face forward, the fields of vision overlap giving stereoscopic vision enabling very precise judgement of distances within pouncing range. Cats are rather nearsighted, although changes in the shape of the lens can compensate for this to some extent. The corneal surface is kept moist and clean by the secretion of the lachrymal glands and the movement of the upper and lower eyelids, as well as the nictitating membrane (third eyelid). The secretions drain away by a minute duct at the inner corner, leading down into the nasal cavity. This is easily blocked, so that disfiguring secretions may run over the fur at the inner corner of the eye.

Ears

Hearing is exceptionally well developed in cats since many rely on perceiving high-pitched squeaks and rustles for locating their prey. The ears are moved and held erect by small muscles in order to scan the surroundings and collect sounds. Accurate location depends on airborne sounds received by the two ears being slightly out of phase, the time difference being used to locate the source. Ear movements are also used to signal to other cats. Sound waves are carried down the external ear to the tympanic membrane and across the middle ear by a chain of ossicles to the cochlea of the inner ear, where sound waves are analysed. Following analysis in the cochlea, sound waves are converted into nerve impulses and are carried to the auditory cortex where they are 'recognized', a process involving learning. A cat thus learns to respond to sounds. It can be taught to respond to its name, and can be called to food. Cats are not so easily trained in this way as dogs, however. The cat's ear is able to register frequencies two octaves higher than a human's but is not so sensitive to frequencies below middle C. At high frequencies cats are more sensitive and can respond to sound of very small intensity. They are also capable of very fine discrimination of the order of $\frac{1}{5}$ tone or better. In all cats acuity falls off with age, and in white cats deafness occurs at an early age due to changes in the cochlea. Blockage of the outer and middle ears also causes deafness.

A second part of the inner ear, the semi-circular canals and ampullae, is concerned with maintaining balance. If a cat is held upside down about eighteen inches (45 cm) off the ground and then dropped, it will succeed in turning over and landing gracefully on all four paws. Failure to do this suggests that the inner ear has been damaged.

In light of low intensity the iris relaxes, and the pupil becomes dilated and round to collect the maximum amount of light.

In strong light the iris constricts and the pupil becomes a vertical slit to exclude unwanted light.

Smell and taste

Cats do not use the sense of smell to track their prey in the way that a dog does; the nose is short and the mucous membrane associated with smell more restricted. The sense of smell is related to feeding, social and sexual activities. Domestic cats possess a small pouch (call Jacobson's organ) in the roof of the mouth lined with receptor cells and although this may be associated with savouring food it is more likely to have social functions. The grimace called 'flehmen' made by wild carnivores and other species in which the lips are pulled back and up, the nose wrinkled and drawn back and the head raised, is occasionally seen in domestic cats scenting the urine of other cats. This curious attitude may allow the scent to reach Jacobson's organ. The sense of taste is limited to the perception of salt, sour, bitter and sweet flavours by the tongue. On the whole, cats like salt but vary greatly in their response to sugar although chocolate is usually liked. Fresh blood, meat or liver usually evoke a very positive response but this is due to the sense of smell rather than taste.

Vibrissae

Cats possess large, stiff, normally slightly curved hairs arranged in rows on either side of the upper lip with smaller tufts elsewhere. These are the vibrissae or whiskers and are brought into action by bundles of muscles so that they stand out from the head. They operate as very sensitive levers, a small movement or touch at the tip being transmitted to the nerve net at the base, setting up a train of impulses which is transmitted by the large nerve leading back to the brain. Vibrissae are used for sensing the immediate environment, touching objects and avoiding obstacles. They are also used in threat displays.

Mouth

The mouth is lined by a moist mucous membrane which is fairly easily damaged but usually heals rapidly. The very specialized tongue takes part, with the teeth, in the process of chewing. It is developed for lapping and curls up at the edges like a spoon to collect liquid from an open surface. Adult cats are unable to suck water from the end of a tube, however. The upper surface of the tongue carries a group of large, cornified papillae which point backwards and feel rough to the touch. These are used for grooming, like a comb. Three principal pairs of salivary glands and many smaller ones in the mucous membrane keep the mouth moist, wash away bacteria and dead cells

With hindlegs flexed ready to launch into a spring, an alert cat stalks its prey, gazing intently forward, vibrissae at the ready.

The curious 'flehmen' reaction in which the lips are drawn back from the teeth with an expression of distaste. It is seen more often in wild animals examining territorial markings left by others of the same species.

(the inner layers are constantly being replaced) and moisten food so that it can be swallowed. Considerable volumes of saliva are produced daily but the water is re-circulated via the digestive system and blood stream. During illness, reduction of the flow of saliva can be very distressing to the cat which is unable to swallow.

The mouth is connected to the stomach by the throat and a long, distensible, muscular tube – the gullet or oesophagus – which passes down behind the heart and lungs. The pharynx (back of the mouth) is also connected to the nasal passages and to the windpipe which lead down the front of the neck to the lungs via the nose or the mouth. Cats can be observed breathing through the mouth when the nasal passages are obstructed. The conjunction of food and air passages has some disadvantages, since liquid, food or vomit can be aspirated into the lungs with fatal consequences. Accidents are most likely to occur when handfeeding young kittens, forcibly dosing an older cat or when giving the cat an anaesthetic on a full stomach. It is very important that cats are denied food overnight when they are to be given an anaesthetic the next day.

Brain

To receive, collate and make use of the mass of sensory information about the environment from eyes, ears, nose, mouth, jaws, vibrissae and skin of the head, a cat requires a complex brain. To this external information must be added information about the cat's own body, the degree of contraction or relaxation of muscles, the position of joints and tendons, information about pressure on skin areas such as the pads of the feet and information about the state of activity of the visceral organs. The relationship of one part to another, particularly the position of the limbs relative to the head and neck, ensures stability and enables the body to move as a unit. Some of this information may enter awareness but much is always below the level of consciousness although it can be raised to the conscious

Above The African wild cat, *Felis libyca,* which inhabits arid scrublands in N. Africa, Asia and S. Europe. Ancestors of this cat were domesticated by the Egyptians and may have given rise to the modern domestic cat. Notice the large ears which aid in locating prey.

Right The wild cat of N. Europe, *Felis sylvestris,* is a forest dweller. An expert climber, it is aggressive and very difficult to domesticate.

The rough tongue with backward-pointing papillae for grooming, the lips and teeth are well shown by this yawning Siamese cat. The guard hairs of the coat and the vibrissae are also apparent.

level when essential for decision making. Thus the brain has to analyse the incoming information and translate it rapidly and effectively into useful actions upon which survival will depend. Muscular movements are co-ordinated by a well-developed cerebellum, while judgements are made in the fairly complex cerebral hemisphere as to the appropriateness of these movements in relation to the needs of the cat. The basal brain stem region is concerned with head reflexes and the control of visceral functions – blood pressure, respiratory movements, temperature regulation, osmoregulation, appetite control and basic sexual behaviour – but it also contains important areas integrating the nervous and endocrine systems. The spinal cord is mainly concerned with local limb and body reflexes, but also relays information up to the brain (via sensory tracts) and down from the brain to the muscles (via motor tracts).

THE SKIN AND COAT

Skin provides a barrier between individual and environment. This barrier must be sensitive to touch, waterproof (since animals cannot afford to lose fluid in an unregulated way) and must be an effective insulator. The skin and fur of a cat are very efficient in meeting these criteria, fur being a particularly good insulator. If the coat is touched on a cold day it will feel cold but the skin beneath the fur feels warm; conversely, when the cat lies in the sun or in front of a hot fire the coat feels hot but the skin feels relatively cool. The thick fur protects the soft skin from abrasions, scratches and bites, and forms a waterproof covering in wet conditions. In the wild the colour of coat has two rather contradictory uses: firstly it makes the cat inconspicuous when stalking its prey so that it 'melts' into its surroundings, and secondly it makes it socially conspicuous and acts as a threat against other predators. The skin of the pads, along with the claws, are specialized both for gripping and for fighting.

Since the coat is so important in domestic and show cats the structure of skin will be described in some detail. In vertical section the skin consists externally of an epidermis formed by many layers of closely packed cells. Some of the innermost cells divide every day to compensate for cells shed from the outer surface. As the cells move outwards they develop a protein – soft keratin – which provides the body with a resistant barrier to water and bacteria. Downgrowths of the epidermis form the basis of the coat, vibrissae, eyelashes and claws. They also form several important kinds of glands: sebaceous glands associated with the roots of hairs whose fatty secretion keep the hair supple, shining and waterproof; sweat glands which are confined to the pads of the paws; mammary glands which provide milk for the kittens; and secretory glands of the chin and forehead which have a special social significance.

The dermis is a supporting and nourishing layer of connective tissue made up of rough, interlacing collagen and slender elastic fibres, embedded in a small amount of jelly-like matrix. All these are manufactured by small cells called fibroblasts. In addition to supporting the epidermis, the dermis can stretch to allow for movements at joints and changes in the shape of the body. Nerves, lymph vessels and blood vessels lie just beneath the epidermis and are associated with the hairs and glands. The developing base of the hair sits in a follicle like a cap, over a dermal papilla containing capillaries; the round hair elongates towards the surface as a result of the division and growth of cells at its base. The cells form a central medullary region with air spaces and pigmented cells, and a thin outer cortex of flattened scale-like cells consisting of hard keratin. When the hair has completed its growth in length it rests, and the blood supply to the base is cut off. It eventually becomes a club-hair and is shed, to be replaced by a new hair growing up from the base of the follicle. Hairs are shed and renewed at regular intervals – spring and autumn in the wild. Although in cats there are not great differences between the summer and winter coats, cats kept in relatively cool conditions have more luxuriant, thicker coats than those kept too warm. Domestication has upset the seasonal rhythm of coat change, so that most domestic cats shed a few hairs all the time, hence the need for constant grooming in longhaired varieties.

The coat consists of slender crimped, or wavy, down or awned-down underhairs. These are covered by coarser overhairs consisting of long, straight, guard hairs (monotrichs) and bent-tipped awn hairs. In most cat varieties hair follicles are arranged in groups of three to five. The primary follicle forming the overhair develops first in the kitten followed by two lateral follicles. Later secondary follicles forming the underhairs are developed. A growing kitten sheds its soft, juvenile coat as it replaces its teeth. The adult coat grows between four and six months, markedly altering the appearance of the kitten. The guard-hairs, like vibrissae, have tactile nerve-endings wound round their base and thus have both a protective and an informative function.

The skin of the pads and tip of the nose are free from hair. The nose is exceptionally sensitive to touch, while the pads are more sensitive to pressure. The epidermis of the pads is very thick and roughened, especially in the hind paws, and provides good friction with the ground for pushing off when running and to prevent slipping when climbing. The glands in the pads secrete sweat when the cat is hot or frightened. The claws are made of sheets of hard keratin and grow continuously from the base, like a nail. Normally they wear down at the same rate as they grow but when a confined cat cannot exercise or scratch on wood the claws may have to be trimmed.

Coat Colour

Coat colour in cats depends on the presence of pigment granules in the epidermal cells. Absence of these granules results in white skin and fur. The pigment which imparts coat colour is called *melanin*, and it is present as two related compounds; *eumelanin* giving black or brown, and *phaeomelanin* giving a yellow or reddish colour to the hair. Eumelanin is derived from an amino acid called tyrosine which is present in the food. A copper-containing enzyme converts this into pigment by a series of stages. Coat colours will therefore not develop normally in cats with a dietary copper deficiency. Phaeomelanin is produced as the result of the presence of another amino acid called tryptophan. Variation in colour throughout the length of the hair is mainly due to the way the pigment is distributed within the hair cells. Tabby hairs are banded yellow

Top left **Female cream longhair.**
Left **Male red self.**
Above **Male blue longhair.** Note the space between the tiny ears, the bold, round eyes and the short muzzle. In this specimen the new coat is not yet fully grown.
Right **A superb red longhair.**

with black or brown tips. They produce the characteristic coat colours of both wild cats and the domestic tabby cat.

Melanin is produced by special cells called melanocytes which secrete the pigment granules into the epidermis, hairs and eyes. Melanocytes are formed in the embryo from cells in the region called the neural crest. During development these migrate first to the head and then the back and finally the belly and limbs. Sometimes this migration is incomplete, giving the cat a white belly and paws, and at other times only a small amount of migration reaches the head, or none at all, resulting in a form called dominant white. When mating a dominant white cat with coloured varieties the offspring will be white, because although the offspring carry colour genes these will be suppressed. When the offspring are bred with each other they will produce a litter having both coloured and white offspring.

In some dominant white cats where the pigment cells have failed to migrate to the inner ear, deafness may result and this may become apparent at any time up to nine months of age. When choosing from a litter of white cats you cannot predict which will turn out to be deaf although some carry a minute patch of grey hair between the eyes, showing that migration of pigment has reached the head. Such cats are never deaf and although they make good pets they would be no use for showing.

THE BLOOD SYSTEM

The circulatory system is based on the typical mammalian double cycle pattern. The heart pumps blood round the pulmonary (lung) circuit where it is oxygenated, then pumps it round the circuit which includes all the other organs. Thick-walled, contractile arteries carry blood at high pressure from the heart and distribute it to fine capillaries which run through the tissues. Here, all exchanges of gases, foods, hormones and other biochemical substances occur. Blood at low pressure is collected into veins and returned to the heart. The circulatory system of the cat is remarkable for the rapid and efficient way in which it can adapt to the requirements of an animal which may be completely still at one moment and performing violent muscular movements the next.

Blood consists of a watery plasma, with dissolved mineral salts, proteins and other materials in transport, in which are suspended platelets, red cells and white cells. Blood clotting occurs by the interaction of platelets and certain plasma proteins in areas of tissue damage such as wounds or bruises. The erythrocytes (red blood cells), contain a red, iron-containing respiratory pigment called haemoglobin and are responsible for transporting oxygen from the lungs to the tissues. They also play a major part in taking excess carbon dioxide back to the lungs. Red blood cells have a limited life in the circulation and are constantly replaced, new cells being formed by active precursor cells dividing and growing in bone marrow. Normal replacement depends on adequate nutrition, particularly supplies of protein, iron, copper, vitamin B_{12} and folic acid. A cat may become anaemic (lacking in red cells) from loss of blood through wounding, from parasitic and other infections or from the toxic effects of drugs which destroy circulating cells and also damage bone marrow. Phenacetin is one of the most dangerous drugs in this respect with aspirin running it a close second. They should never be given to cats. White blood cells are responsible for maintaining the body's defence, particularly against bacteria and viruses, and are formed in bone marrow and lymphoid tissue. 'Memory' cells capable of initiating the production of antibodies may last one or more years thus providing the cat with active immunity.

THE DIGESTIVE SYSTEM

Cats' digestive systems are adapted to flesh eating and are short and simple because such a high proportion of their food can be utilized. The food is swallowed in quite sizeable pieces and is held in the stomach for between one and five hours. Here it is pounded by the stomach muscles and mixed with an enzyme which breaks down protein until it is reduced to a gruel-like consistency. As the dissolved or finely particulate mass is formed it is passed on to the small intestine where digestive breakdown of proteins, fats and carbohydrates is completed with the aid of enzyme-containing digestive juices from the pancreas and intestinal wall, and bile from the liver. The soluble products of digestion – amino acids, fatty acids and glycerol, simple sugars, vitamins and mineral salts – pass into the portal veins and are carried to the liver. The liver is a vital organ of great importance to many metabolic processes. Food substances are stored in it and released as required. Plasma proteins are manufactured there and toxic substances, either ingested or produced in other regions of the body, are dealt with so that they become harmless and can be excreted. In this last respect the liver of the cat seems to be less efficient than that of rats or humans. Substances such as the food preservative benzoic acid are tolerated by humans but are toxic to the cat. One of the reasons why aspirin and phenacetin are so dangerous to a cat is that they are poorly detoxicated and therefore build up to damaging levels in the blood although similar dose levels are harmless to human beings.

Water, indigestible material and the remains of discarded cells from the gut lining (which is renewed about every third day in the cat), pass on into the large intestine. Here, some bacterial action occurs but it is of little importance compared with that in herbivores and some omnivores. The main function of the large intestine is to absorb water and possibly some mineral salts. Owing to the small volume of residual matter, meat-fed cats void the faeces relatively infrequently, not even daily. It has been observed, however, that the domestic cat has a larger gut than the European wild cat, so that introducing a mixed, omnivorous diet to a natural carnivore may be having an adaptive effect.

The kidneys produce a more concentrated urine than in other species of domesticated animal, possibly because domestic cats originated from species living in hot, near-desert conditions. Because of the carnivorous diet the kidneys also have to deal with relatively large amounts of nitrogenous waste matter, sulphur and phosphorus.

THE REPRODUCTIVE ORGANS AND REPRODUCTION

The male cat has paired testes which, during development, descend from their position in the abdominal cavity to the scrotal sacs, where they can be felt as solid, oval structures under the skin. This occurs either while the kitten is still in the uterus, or in early postnatal life. The testes produce sperms and the male hormone *testosterone*. The sperms undergo maturation on their journey down the long epididymis – a tube coiled over the surface of the testes. The sperms are then led back into the abdomen via the vas deferens, where nutritive and other secretions (including valeric acid which gives cats their characteristic odour) are added from the prostrate and urethral glands to form semen. Small quantities of semen are ejaculated at coitus. In some tom cats one or both testes may fail to descend, making him completely or partially infertile. Since this defect can be inherited, one should not use such a cat at stud. Removal of the testes leads to regression of the sex glands and loss of the 'catty' odour.

Female cats have paired ovaries lying on either side of the vertebrae in the abdominal cavity just behind the kidneys. In adults, they secrete the female hormone *oestrogen*. Twenty-six hours after copulation, which stimulates the release of hormones from the pituitary gland, the ovaries expel several (usually four) ova. These are collected in the funnel of the coiled fallopian tube within which they are fertilized by the male's sperms. Sperms are ejaculated by the male into the female vagina, and take about two days to swim up the uterus and fallopian tubes. Once fertilized, the egg cells develop in the fallopian tube for five to six days and divide forming blastocysts which pass into the uterus. Meanwhile the ovaries secrete *progesterone*, a hormone responsible for distributing, implanting and maintaining the blastocysts in the uterus. This phase is critical. When only one kitten is born it is likely that the rest of the litter was lost at this stage. By the thirty-fifth day the embryo, although only $\frac{1}{5}$ inch (5mm) long, has a recognizable shape and after this time begins to grow more quickly. The ovaries cease to secrete progesterone by the forty-second to forty-eighth day, and any severe disturbance (such as a pregnant cat falling from a height) or food shortage at this time can cause a cat to give premature birth to the kittens – this is probably a protective mechanism to ensure survival of the mother. Progesterone production is then taken over by the placenta until the end of pregnancy, which ranges between sixty-one and sixty-nine days, but normally sixty-five.

Above Tortoiseshell-and-white longhair.
Left Tortoiseshell longhair.
Right A champion male brown tabby longhair glares suspiciously at the camera.

Behaviour

TERRITORY

Many animals spend their lives in a limited area called the home range, over which they usually travel in pursuit of their routine activities. For carnivores such as cats, and for many other animals also, part (or sometimes the whole) of the home range becomes a territory, particularly during the breeding season. The territory has strictly defined, marked boundaries and is stoutly defended against neighbouring individuals and transients (young or displaced animals) of the same species. The territory may be occupied by a single animal, a breeding pair, a family group or a pack, depending on the social habits of the particular animal concerned. In some species, the numbers within a territory vary with the time of year. The size of the territory depends on the size and habits of the animal – a pride of lions may occupy ten square miles or more (more than sixteen square kilometres) and a wild cat half a square mile (0·8 square kilometres) or less – but it depends much more on the density of the food supply.

Most wild animals' waking hours are spent in gathering food, so naturally they do not travel further than is necessary to fill their stomachs. Territories of predators such as cats are at least four times the area occupied by equivalent sized herbivores (grazers). Thus, there are fewer predators than prey in any particular area. A cat's territory is increased when game is short and it may then risk trespassing on its neighbour's ground. Conversely, when food is plentiful territories contract and, under normal circumstances, the population density of the species increases. The geographical location of the territory may vary

A mother cat relaxing in the den watches her kittens practise co-ordination of movement in play.

seasonally, a cat moving with game up into mountains in summer and down into valleys in winter. The territory of a wild or feral cat (a domestic cat that has gone wild) includes important facilities besides food; the more desirable the territory the better these other facilities will be. They include a well-hidden principal den where the cat can relax, sleep and feel totally secure. The young are usually born in this den and may also be reared there. A number of subsidiary dens (comfortable resting places or temporary refuges) are distributed conveniently over the territory. A water-hole or drinking point is an important feature visited daily. Points for urination or defaecation (usually separate) are always some distance from dens since these might otherwise indicate the den's position to a larger predator. These points, especially those for urination, are also used to demarcate the limits of the territory since scent is deposited and renewed daily. In this connection it is interesting to note that the European wild cat does not bury its faeces as does the domestic cat. Warning marks are also made by the cat rubbing special glands in the skin of its chin and forehead on trees, posts and stones; by spraying from anal glands (especially by the male); and by scratching trees or posts with the foreclaws while standing on the hindlegs. All these territorial boundary marks are regularly renewed as the cat normally behaves in a very routine way, following the same path daily as can be seen from paw prints in mud or snow. The domestic cat retains nearly all the behavioural patterns associated with territory, and these can be readily observed in your cat's everyday activities.

SOCIAL SYSTEM

Small wild cats occupy a territory singly, or more usually as a pair, rearing their young within its confines. Lions which have been more extensively studied than other wild cat species live in an extended family group called a pride which contains a dominant male, two or three females (one of which may have ceased breeding) and one or two litters of cubs. Young adults are generally pushed out of the pride when they are eighteen months to three years old, by which time they will have been trained in the methods of hunting and self-defence. In many ways domestic cats behave like lions. A tom cat, left to his own devices, will gather a harem of one or two queens into his territory within which the group will live harmoniously often sharing the business of suckling, rearing and training the kittens. Domestic cats, although sometimes possessive of their kittens, will usually readily adopt other cat's kittens or even young of other species, such as puppies and rabbits. The tom remains strongly dominant; other younger males invading the territory are rapidly chased off and kittens are only tolerated while they are still juvenile. Mature offspring, especially males, wander off and establish their own territories and any that remain are unusually submissive and are not allowed any opportunity of mating with the harem's queens when the latter are in season. The pack system adopted by wolves and dogs involves a much greater degree of co-operation in the hunt for food for they tend to live in relatively large communities. Thus the contrasting habits of domestic dogs and cats may be traced to fundamental differences in their social behaviour.

Apart from the hierarchy among toms during mating, social order and rank are not firmly adhered to among domestic cats; first one adult then another will take precedence in feeding. Some cats prefer their own individual sleeping quarters, others are content to lie anywhere – even with the family dog. Individual preferences should be observed and catered for. Problems can arise, however, when over-breeding results in the overpopulation of a relatively small area, from which rejected animals or young adults cannot escape to form new territories. In such conditions some animals, usually males but sometimes females, are prevented from eating until the others have had their fill. The outcast may eventually sicken and die. In other instances serious fighting may break out because the subordinate cat has no means of escape and no safe place to retreat to. Fighting in such circumstances can be prevented by removing animals at risk, seeing that there is plenty of food for all and reducing the population. To prevent over-population, you should limit the number of cats that you keep. Three (perhaps a tom and two queens) is a safe number for a medium-sized house with a garden, and two is the maximum for a flat. Fighting can

Three more beautiful
examples of longhaired
cats.
Above A seal colour-
point. Colourpoints
were produced by
selective breeding of
Siamese and longhairs.
Left Self lilac. These
cats have recently been
granted recognition
by the Governing
Council of the Cat
Fancy.
Right Champion male
silver tabby.

THE EXPRESSION OF EMOTION

also be prevented and discouraged by the sheer dominance or will power of the human being whom the cats accept as their master.

Emotional states are signalled very clearly by carnivores in the knowledge that members of their own species are, because of their acute vision, easily able to read these signals. Signals are made primarily by the whole attitude of the body: tense and ready for action; relaxed and contented; or suppliant and demanding attention. The position and movements of the head and tail of a domestic cat are especially significant and are carefully observed by dogs and human beings as well as by other cats. Anxiety or fear are expressed by dilation of the pupils, the eyes rapidly scanning the surroundings, the ears flattened and the tail held low – signals which indicate submission to dominant cats or other animals. Fear signals may develop into warning signals rather than submission; adrenalin is secreted, hair rises along the spine and tail, the back is arched, the claws extend and the tail is held high and stiff, or slowly and deliberately

Above **Kittens will choose their own places for relaxation.**
Left **The doubtful kitten tries to frighten off the dominant intruder by a threat display intended to make it look bigger, with arched back and bristling fur.**
Right **The aggressive stance, retracted lips and dilated pupils of the adult cat facing the camera is a characteristic threat display warning the other cat not to approach.**

Top left The cat, confronted by an inquisitive dog, feels threatened but can still retreat a short distance.
Left Having retreated as far as possible, the cat turns on the dog with a threatening expression, pupils dilated, ears flattened and paw ready to strike.
Above Finally the display turns into an attack, with a noisy spit and striking paw, claws extended. The dog retreats rapidly.

lashed from side to side – all this is intended to make the cat appear larger, and therefore potentially more dangerous, than it really is. As the threat develops the lips are drawn back from the teeth and the eyes glare. The cat growls and hisses and finally explodes in a ferocious spit. The cat appears to be about to launch an attack on the intruder but if confronted by a larger or more determined animal undeterred by the spitting display the cat, unless cornered, will take refuge in flight to the nearest safe point – usually high up on a ledge or in a tree. A dominant tom will chase another off his patch and a queen will stand her ground to defend her kittens but otherwise the unsuccessful threat will end in rapid flight. A cat in an excited condition of fear will attack if cornered or when defending its young. It is important to avoid going too close to a cat in this state. In other words, one should avoid entering the 'flight distance' – usually about one yard (one metre) – when the cat must take action, its warning threats having failed to deter the attacker. The cat will then launch itself at the attacker who is liable to suffer severe scratches and bites. If the cat is wild, feral

or unfamiliar with its surroundings it may actually dash itself against the bars of a cage in an attempt to increase the flight distance between itself and what it considers to be its attacker. This should be avoided at all costs as the cat may damage itself and at the very least suffer from shock and exhaustion following the episode.

A word of warning must be given here. Cat scratches and bites must always be regarded as potentially dangerous. If you handle strange cats frequently you should have anti-tetanus injections maintained by regular booster doses. Bites of the puncture type are difficult to wash clean, however much care is taken. If you or any animal you own are bitten, wash the wounds using plenty of a non-toxic antiseptic solution. Signs of inflammation must be taken seriously and reported as soon as practical to the doctor (for yourself) or the vet (for your animals). A dangerous or frightened cat is best controlled by covering and rapidly rolling it in a large bath towel or small blanket. The cat will put out its claws which become hooked on to the thick material and it will also bite this rather than its handler.

It should be allowed to recover in a perfectly quiet, warm, dimly lit place.

Even wild cats express pleasure and satisfaction, the purr is a perfect expression of relaxed satisfaction and well being. This state occurs when the well-fed cat is 'at home', stretched out in front of a fire, sitting on the lap of its favourite human being or in its basket feeding its kittens. Alternate contraction and relaxation of the forepaws and 'padding on the spot' often accompany purring and resemble the movements made by kittens during suckling.

Play is essential for the proper development of young animals. When playing, kittens learn to co-ordinate vision and movement, to judge distances, to spring, pounce, run and climb – activities of value in later life for survival, food hunting and territory keeping. Threat and pleasure expressions are practised on other kittens in the litter and 'tried out' on adults of the group. Play is actively encouraged by the attentive mother cat as a part of the elaborate training she gives her young. Her attitudes and signals are constantly watched and

copied by her kittens. Kittens and young cats are noted for their inquisitive behaviour; they continually explore, learning to recognize and extend their living space, building up impressions and information for future use. In later life cats, like most other animals including human beings, lose much of their investigatory behaviour and gradually replace it by a strongly developed routine. Removal of a cat to new surroundings reactivates investigatory behaviour straight away, however, and the cat cannot rest until it has examined every corner of its new home, including all those cupboards and drawers which might make useful new dens or refuges. Sometimes dissatisfaction with the new territory causes the cat to try to find its way back to its old home. Journeys of up to ten miles (sixteen kilometres) are commonly made in this way – on occasion much further. There has been much speculation as to how the cat manages to return to its old home, especially when the journey to the new home was made in a covered basket. A factor sometimes forgotten in these cases is that cats, especially country

Above Play by kittens enacts the situations and develops the skills required for hunting their prey in adult life. *Right* Kittens are more inquisitive than adult cats and continually explore their surroundings.

cats, often have an extensive knowledge of the area around them and are more able to recognize their surroundings than human beings give them credit for. An amorous tom can cover ten miles (sixteen kilometres) in a night visiting farms. Town cats are much less likely to return to their old homes unless the distance is less than a mile (1·6 kilometres).

COMMUNICATION

Cats communicate with one another and with human beings and express their emotional state by a number of calls in addition to the growling and spitting and the satisfied purring mentioned above. Most of these calls are associated with sexual activity in adults or with communication with kittens. The frequency and loudness of vocalization vary greatly. Siamese are notoriously noisy while other breeds simply go through the motion of opening and shutting their mouths, making very little sound. Tom cats growl and spit at each other ferociously when defending a territory or a queen in season and both sexes may mew briefly to indicate a need such as a drink of milk, or a door or window being opened for them. When they are in season many queens, especially Siamese, utter long, wailing cries termed 'calling' which are used to attract the tom. During successful coitus the female gives a tremendous shriek which can be quite alarming when heard at dead of night. It is uncertain whether this cry represents pleasure or pain. Queens communicate with their kittens by short, purr-like calls on a rising note from about the time their eyes open. (Kittens are deaf at birth.) In the absence of the queen kittens remain quiet in their nest but when she returns, or they are disturbed by handling, they utter high pitched mews to which the queen is very sensitive. If she can hear a mewing kitten she will search until she finds it, then carry it back to the nest.

ADAPTATION TO THE HUMAN ENVIRONMENT

Of all animals, dogs and cats have adapted best to domestication, that is, living with and eventually becoming almost totally dependent on human beings. Cats have simply taken over human habitations and their precincts as their territory, dominated by the tom and to a lesser extent by the queens, especially when the latter have kittens. Both will chase strange cats off the premises with speed and efficiency – unless the straying visitor is very young and does not constitute a threat. The degree of acceptance of human beings into the family unit of the cat is very variable and there is evidence that 'wildness' has a physical basis. Thus the offspring of wild or feral cats are extremely difficult – even dangerous – to handle and make poor pets although they are good rodent eliminators. Nor is this wildness overcome by hand-rearing the kittens, even from a very early age. It is probable that the domestication of cats between two and three thousand or more years ago, involving the continuous selection of those best adapted to living with man, was likewise accompanied by heritable changes in behaviour and temperament. Those cats which were most easily handled would be kept and would probably breed more readily in association with human beings. This association has caused the domestic cat to lose some of its independence, however, since the very traits which enabled it to compete and survive so successfully became relatively unimportant. The domestic cat is less suspicious, allows the human to take up a dominant role, is more easily caught and handled and is less able to acquire its food by hunting, although this latter role has tended to be encouraged by breeding good mousers at least until very recent times.

When a human being assumes the dominant role over the cats in the home territory he or she then becomes the provider of shelter (the den) and food. Where the territory is very restricted, as in a flat or cathouse, the dominant human being must provide suitable areas for drinking, urination and defaecation, which the cat marks with scent or by scratching. In many homes it is noticeable that one particular piece of furniture is chosen as the 'scratch post'; often a convenient table leg of softish wood, such as that of a kitchen table. The more confined the cat is, the more essential it is to provide a proper territory in miniature. It has been a matter for speculation as to how the cat regards the human being within its territory. Queens often transfer their normal attachment from the dominant tom to a single human being taking little notice, except in an absent-minded way, of other members of the human family. The queen will go to this person and make known her requirements for food, water or for a door to be opened. The rapport existing between these individuals is often of a high order, and the human being has no doubt at all as to what the animal requires. The rapport with the tom is usually of a different nature. He is more independent, and although he takes to 'family' life he still insists on marking his territory and will treat newcomers with considerable reserve. Another interesting point about domestication is the way in which the cat casually and happily accepts other familiar animals such as dogs or parrots within the territory but will chase away strangers of the same species, especially if they appear on the margins of the territory.

COURTSHIP AND MATING BEHAVIOUR

Healthy, female kittens may become sexually mature under six months of age, but usually at seven to eight months. They often continue to grow while producing their first litter. Although male kittens grow faster than females from about ten weeks of age onwards, they do not mature before nine months and sometimes not until fifteen months of age. The tom will continue to grow for about another year but it should be noted that grossly overweight cats make poor breeding animals.

The onset of sexual interest becomes apparent in the queen in late January to early April in the year after she was born, before which time toms take no particular interest in her. With increasing length of daylight the region of the brain called the hypothalamus is stimulated, and this triggers off the release of gonadotrophic hormones from the pituitary gland. These pass via the blood stream to the ovary where they stimulate active growth of ovarian follicles. At the same time the ovary secretes the hormone called oestrogen which prepares the uterus (womb) for implantation. Oestrogens also arrive at the brain via the blood stream where they activate sexual behaviour. Sexual behaviour in the female cat is very stereotyped, following the same pattern time after time. The oestrogens stimulate the glands near the vaginal orifice to secrete an odorous substance imperceptible to human beings but highly attractive to tom cats. In the preparatory period the queen will reject the tom's advances by striking at him with the unsheathed claws of her forepaws, growling and moving away if he attempts to mount. This phase is over quickly (after one to two days) following which, her mood changes dramatically.

In mating, the tom mounts the queen, grasping the skin at the back of the neck in his teeth and holding her between his forepaws. The queen's tail is deflected and intromission follows.

She begins rubbing her head, crouching low on her forelimbs, elevating her pelvic region, deflecting her tail and performing treading movements with the hind limbs. She purrs and when the tom mounts, she accepts him at once.

In mounting, the tom takes a firm neck hold with his teeth and grips the queen's body between his forelegs. He executes intromission with a rapid thrusting movement and ejaculation of a small quantity of semen occurs at once. There is no 'tie' as there is in the dog. The queen utters a single, blood-curdling scream then violently disengages herself and rolls over to and fro on her back, alternating with frenzied licking of the vulva. During this important 'after-reaction' the tom retreats to a safe distance and watches her cautiously. If he attempts to approach her he will be met with a furious growl accompanied by a blow from a forepaw with claws extended. The after-reaction gradually diminishes in intensity and within a quarter to one hour the queen begins to court the tom once more, purring and rubbing, ready to mate again.

The number of intromissions and degree of excitement required seem to vary from one queen to another, and a breeder should take care to leave the tom with the queen long enough to ensure ovulation. When more than one tom is present the males will form a ring around the queen, watching her from a respectful distance. She will mate at first with the dominant tom but sometimes later matings at the same heat will be with sub-dominants. The queen may also show aversion to certain toms, which she constantly rejects even though in full heat. Furthermore some toms, however good as show specimens, seem too nervous of the queen to mount her. A breeder should therefore make sure that the whole ritual is carried through to completion. Once the mated queen passes into the next phase she will totally reject the tom; this happens twenty-four to forty-eight hours after successful mating. If mating has been unsuccessful, or if the queen has not been mated, she will normally remain in oestrus (on heat) for four to six days. Indeed, if her living area is near to that of an active tom, she becomes very frustrated and may appear to call incessantly. Normally, however, there is a quiescent period of about two weeks before she starts calling again.

The mother cat examines the wet, newborn kitten still attached to the after-birth (placenta) by the umbilical cord. Normally the cord is bitten through by the cat when the kitten is born.

Right Notice the large head, short nose and closed eyes of these kittens which are only a few days old. They make weak, scrabbling movements towards the smell of milk.

Below A mother cat has been disturbed by the photographer and is alert to defend her young. Notice the nipple on the right of the suckling kitten.

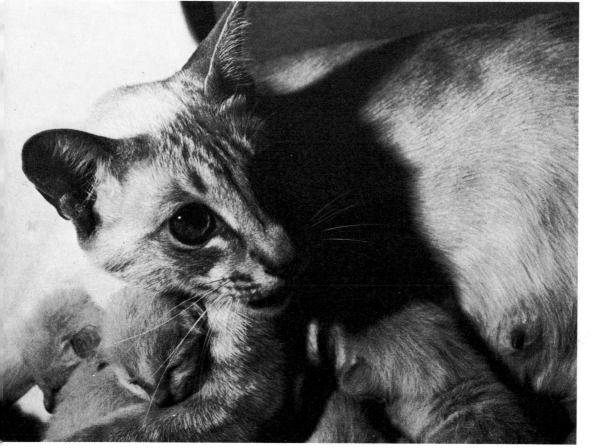

Choosing a cat

Having decided to share your life with a cat, you must next decide upon the kind of cat you prefer. This is often a difficult task, for there are many recognized varieties of *Felis catus*. Pedigree cats may first be divided into longhairs, semi-longhairs and shorthairs, and the latter may be subdivided into British shorthairs and foreign shorthairs, the popular Siamese being one variety in the latter classification. Many of the shorthairs, including the Siamese, occur in colour variations which thus increase still further the problem which the would-be owner must solve.

Once you have decided upon the variety of cat you wish to own, with the help of the descriptions given in this chapter, you should consider whether you wish perhaps to breed the variety or join a club and show a neutered specimen. Finally, if you are interested in breeding you must make up your mind whether you wish to keep breeding queens or own a stud. None of these decisions should be made lightly, for keeping an animal or perhaps several animals is a prospect which should be viewed with a deep sense of responsibility. It is true that one cat, or even a small number of cats, may be fed and housed without difficulty, but to maintain the perfect health so essential in a show animal the provision of a balanced diet is important. Of course, if you merely wish to keep a pedigree cat as a pet it is generally sufficient to treat it as a member of the family, sharing the family table and, on occasions, the family bed. Conversely, where several cats are kept for show and for breeding, the question of housing and proper feeding should be considered with some care.

All of these questions are adequately dealt with in other parts of this book, but it may be worth mentioning here the special problems of keeping a stud cat. A mature stud cannot lead a healthy, happy and otherwise normal life unless he is given the opportunity to serve an adequate number of queens. Few breeders, except the very largest, have sufficient queens of their own and this means that queens visiting the stud for mating will normally constitute their main source of income. Unless the stud is a champion, or is in other ways well known, he is unlikely to attract enough visiting females, and it follows that to keep an undistinguished male as a stud is to constrain him to a life of discontent. On no account should an entire male be kept unless his owner has good reasons to think that he will be a popular stud, for an entire male pet cat will go out to seek his own female company, siring unwanted kittens in the process. Such a course is not possible with a pedigree cat used at public stud, for a cat with torn ears and other inevitable damage is unlikely to impress the owners of visiting queens or, for that matter, the show judges. It may be useful at this point to outline the system used here in the classification of domestic cats. Fundamental differences such as longhair, British shorthair, foreign shorthair or Siamese are referred to as *breeds*. Divisions within each breed such as black, tortoiseshell and chinchilla are termed *varieties*. The *variety number* is the number given to the variety when it achieves recognition from the Governing Council of the Cat Fancy.

LONGHAIRED (PERSIAN) CATS

In the eyes of many cat lovers the longhaired cats are judged to be the most beautiful of the pedigree varieties. All longhairs must conform as closely as possible to the same general type in which the body is massive and cobby, with plenty of bone and substance, low on the leg and without any trace of coarseness. The head must be round and broad, with plenty of width between the ears which should be small, neat and well covered. The cat must have a short nose, full cheeks and a broad muzzle.

Black
VARIETY 1
Coat: lustrous, raven-black to the roots and free from rustiness, shading, white hairs or

Female blue-eyed white longhair. Still rather long in the nose, this beautiful variety is rapidly improving and is becoming increasingly popular on the show bench.

markings of any kind. **Eyes**: large, round and wide open, copper or deep orange without a green rim. **Tail**: short, broad and well furnished. Black kittens often exhibit a poor coat until they are five or six months old, the coat being grey or rusty in parts, and sometimes freely speckled with white hairs. Kittens exhibiting these faults should not be automatically rejected as they often turn into beautiful adults.

Blue-eyed White and Orange-eyed White
VARIETIES 2 and 2a
Coat: pure white without marks or shades of any kind. **Eyes**: deep blue, orange or copper.

Odd-eyed White
VARIETY 2b
Coat: pure white. **Eyes**: orange and blue.

Blue
VARIETY 3
The blue longhair is said by some to be the finest example of longhaired cat, although some of the best blacks and orange-eyed whites come close to the blue in perfection. **Coat**: any shade of blue is permitted, but it must be sound throughout. **Head**: surrounded by a full frill. **Eyes**: deep orange or copper. **Ears**: generously tufted.

Red Tabby
VARIETY 9
Coat: deep, rich red with the tabby markings clearly defined and continuing on the chest, tail and legs. **Eyes**: large, round and of deep copper.

Red Self
VARIETY 4
Coat: luxuriant as in all longhairs; deep,

rich red without markings. **Eyes:** deep copper. It is extremely difficult to breed a red self without the slightest trace of tabby markings and the kittens of this variety always carry ghost tabby marks which, it is hoped, will fade out by the time the cat reaches adulthood. Red selfs often grow to a truly massive size and look wonderful if they are of the correct colour.

Cream
VARIETY 5
Coat: pure, sound cream throughout. The common fault with creams is that they have a coat colour which is *hot* or too red. **Eyes:** must be round, large and a deep copper colour.

Tortoiseshell
VARIETY 11
Identical in type with the general longhair specification. **Coat:** in three colours; black, red and cream, well broken into patches, particularly on the face. The colours must be rich and bright and a concentration of any one colour is considered a fault. Tortoiseshells, like all coloured cats, exist in genetic dilutions in which the red may appear as a rich cream while the black colour may be transformed by the Maltese dilution factor into blue. (The Maltese dilution factor is due to a recessive gene which causes black to appear as blue, and also converts red to cream.)

Tortoiseshell-and-white
VARIETY 12
Coat: the three colours, black, red and cream to be well distributed, broken and interspersed with white.

Blue-cream
VARIETY 13
Coat: blue and cream softly intermingled giving a pastel effect with neither colour predominant. The intermingling to be continued on the face.

Brown Tabby
VARIETY 8
Coat: rich, tawny sable with delicate, black pencillings running down the face, and the cheeks crossed with two or three distinct swirls. The chest should be crossed by two unbroken narrow lines or necklaces, and butterfly marks must appear prominently on the shoulders. The front of the legs must be striped regularly from the toes upwards and the saddle and sides must have deep bands running down them. **Eyes:** hazel or copper. **Tail:** regularly ringed.

Chinchilla
VARIETY 10
Among the loveliest of longhairs. **Coat:** pure white undercoat with the coat on the back, flanks and ears tipped with black. The hairs on the tail should be similarly tipped. A genetic dilution exists in which the black tipping is apparent as blue. Recognition has not, as yet, been granted to the blue chinchilla. A perfectly marked chinchilla appears to glow like sparkling silver. The legs may be very slightly shaded with silver but the chin, ear tufts, stomach and chest must be pure white. Tabby markings, or a brown or cream tinge are faults. The tip of the nose should be brick-red, and the skin visible on the eyelids and pads should be black or dark brown. **Head:** less typical of the longhair roundness so perfectly displayed by the blues and the blacks, but this failing will be overcome in time and does not detract from the wistful and faery loveliness of this variety. **Eyes:** expressive emerald or blue-green.

Smoke
VARIETY 6
This is a cat of contrast. **Coat:** undercolour as white as possible with the tips of the hairs shading to black. The dark points are most defined on the back, head and feet; the light points on the frill, flanks and ear tufts. Once again the Maltese dilution produces a blue smoke, in which blue appears in place of black. **Eyes:** orange or copper.

Silver Tabby
VARIETY 7
Coat: ground colour should be pure silver with clearly defined jet-black markings free of any brown tinge. **Eyes:** green or hazel.

Colourpoint
VARIETY 13b
These lovely cats were bred by judicious crossing of Siamese with longhairs. The initial crossing produces progeny having a short, black coat and if these kittens are mated together or to others of their kind a

One of the most beautiful longhaired breeds, the chinchilla shows a superb contrast of colour with its vivid green eyes and its snowy coat tipped with black.

proportion of the second generation (F_2) progeny will be longhairs, some of which may exhibit the well-known Siamese colour distribution. The usual method of early breeding is to mate the first generation (F_1) progeny back to a parent as by this method a greater probability of obtaining longhair kittens with Siamese markings exists. **Coat:** long, thick and soft in texture with a typically Siamese body colour, i.e. cream, glacial white or ivory, depending upon whether the points colour is seal, blue or chocolate. **Points:** must be dense and the body shading, which appears in normal Siamese as tracings, must be the same colour as the points. **Head and general type:** longhair and in no sense Siamese. **Eyes:** deep blue. This quality has so far been difficult to obtain other than in outstanding specimens. **Tail:** short and full, free from kinking and of the same colour as the points.

Bicolour
VARIETY 12a
Coat: any solid colour and white. The patches of colour must be clear, even and well distributed. The face should be patched with colour and white. **Eyes:** deep orange or copper.

BRITISH SHORTHAIRED CATS
The typical British shorthaired cat has a well-knit body and tail giving the appearance of power, stamina and activity. The chest is full and broad and the tail thick at the root, well set and of good proportion to

Left Bicolour longhair.
These cats are difficult
to breed to perfection.
Below Blacks are ever
popular, and this is a
fine example of the
British shorthaired
variety.

Like its longhaired
counterpart, the bi-
colour shorthair is very
good natured.

the body size. The legs are well built and of good proportion to the body, with neat, well-rounded feet. The head is broad between the ears, with the cheeks well developed and a short nose and face, although not as short as in the longhairs. The ears must be short but not wide at the base, and rounded at the tips. The coat is short, fine and close lying, but rather harsh or hard to the touch, unlike that of the longhairs. The shorthair cat's general condition must be hard and muscular.

Blue-eyed White
VARIETY 14
Coat: pure white, untinged with yellow. Eyes: very deep sapphire-blue.

Orange-eyed White
VARIETY 14a
Coat: as in the blue-eyed variety. Eyes: golden, orange or copper. The eyes in all the British shorthair varieties must be large, round and well opened.

Odd-eyed White
VARIETY 14b
Coat: as in the blue-eyed variety. Eyes: orange and blue.

Black
VARIETY 15
Coat: jet-black down to the roots with no rusty tinge or white hairs. Eyes: deep copper or orange with no trace of green.

Blue
VARIETY 16
Coat: light to medium blue. Very level in colour with no tabby markings, shading or white.

Bicolour
VARIETY 31
Coat: any solid colour and white; the patches of colour to be clear and evenly distributed. Not more than two-thirds of the coat should be coloured and not more than one half should be white. The face should be patched with colour, and a white blaze is a desirable feature. Tabby markings, a long tail, brindling within the colour patches and green eyes are considered to be faults. **Eyes:** deep orange, yellow or copper.

Blue-cream
VARIETY 28
Coat: short and fine in texture with the colours softly mingled and not patchy. **Eyes:** copper, orange or yellow with no trace of green.

Cream
VARIETY 17
Coat: rich cream, evenly coloured, free from bars and without any white. **Eyes:** copper or orange.

Silver Tabby
VARIETY 18
Coat: ground colour must be clear silver, and the dense black markings must be distinct and unmingled with the ground colour. No white markings are allowed. A clearly marked butterfly design should appear on the shoulders and typical oyster-shaped rings on the sides. One or more black necklaces must be present. **Eyes:** hazel or orange. **Tail:** ringed with black.

Red Tabby
VARIETY 19
Coat: ground colour red, with the usual tabby markings a denser shade of red unmixed with the ground colour. **Eyes:** hazel or orange.

Brown Tabby
VARIETY 20
Coat: ground colour rich sable or brown, uniform throughout and without any white. Very dense black markings. **Eyes:** orange,

hazel, deep yellow or green.

Spotted Tabby
VARIETY 30
Coat: in this variety spotting is the first essential, other qualities being of somewhat secondary importance. The spots may be round, oblong or rosette-shaped and all of these are considered to be of equal merit providing they are clear and distinct with no tendency to run into the ground colour. Any uniform and attractive ground colour is accepted and the spots may be of any colour which harmonizes with the ground colour. **Eyes:** similarly, the colour must harmonize with the colour of the coat. Stripes and bars (except on the face and head) and any tendency to brindling are faults.

Mackerel Tabby
VARIETY 26
A sub-variety of the spotted tabby in which the spots are replaced by rings which should be as narrow and as numerous as possible, running perpendicular to the spine. Necklaces and a ringed tail must be present.

Tortoiseshell
VARIETY 21
Coat: black and red well balanced and each colour as brilliant as possible. No white. Colour patches to be well defined with no merging, brindling or tabby markings. The legs, feet, tail and ears to be as well patched as the body. A red blaze on the face is desirable. **Eyes:** orange, copper or hazel.

Tortoiseshell-and-white
VARIETY 22
Coat: black and red on white, equally balanced. All the colours to be brilliant and free from brindling or tabby markings. The tricolour patches should cover the top of the head, ears and cheeks as well as the back, tail and part of the flanks. A white blaze is desirable. **Eyes:** orange, copper or hazel.

Manx
VARIETY 25
Taillessness, height of hind quarters, shortness of back and depth of flank are essential in the manx cat as only with this combination is the desired rabbit-like or hopping gait possible. The rump should be as round as an orange. In the finest specimens

An alert mackerel tabby shorthair. Its mackerel markings distinguish it from the spotted tabbies. This variety exists in both silver and brown forms.

taillessness is absolute, a hollow appearing where the tail normally protrudes in other cats. **Coat**: colour is optional but should harmonize with the similarly optional eye colour. Manx cats exhibiting tortoiseshell, bicolour or any other recognized non-self coloration should conform to the general standards specified for each combination, but colour is only taken into account when separating otherwise equally good specimens. The coat is double, i.e. soft and open like that of a rabbit, with a soft, thick undercoat.

FOREIGN SHORTHAIRED CATS
Russian Blue
VARIETY 16a
Coat: clear, medium blue, even throughout; in maturity, free from tabby markings or patches. The coat is doubled in this unique variety so that it possesses a distinct, silvery sheen. The texture must be short, thick and very fine, standing up soft and silky like seal skin. **Head**: ideally a short

wedge with a flat skull, straight forehead and nose forming an angle. The whisker pads must be pronounced and prominent. **Eyes**: vivid green, set wide apart and almond shaped. **Ears**: large and pointed, wide at the base and set vertically on the head instead of diverging as in the Siamese. The skin of the ears must be thin and translucent with very little inside hair. **Legs**: long; must terminate in small, oval feet. White or tabby markings, cobby or heavy build, squareness of head and Siamese-type or yellow coloration in the eyes are faults. **Tail**: fairly long and tapering.

Abyssinian
VARIETY 23
The Abyssinian cat should be slim and dainty and certainly neither large nor coarse. **Coat**: ruddy brown ticked with black or dark brown. Multiple ticking, consisting of two or even three bands of colour on each hair is an advantage. No bars or other markings are allowed except that a

British shorthaired cats must conform to a general standard in which the well-knit, muscular body gives the appearance of power and stamina.
Above A young silver tabby.
Left Cream.
Right The ever-popular blue.

dark spine line will not detract from an otherwise fine specimen. The inside of the forelegs and belly should be of a tint harmonizing with the coat colour, preference being given to apricot or orange-brown. There should be an absence of bars or other markings on the head, tail, face and chest and in particular as little white as possible should appear on the throat, chest and belly. **Head**: a medium wedge with sharp, comparatively large ears, wide at the base. **Eyes**: green, yellow or hazel. Must be large, bright and expressive. **Tail**: fairly long and tapering. The small feet should have black pads, the black colour extending up the back of the hind legs.

Red Abyssinian
VARIETY 23a
Identical to the brown variety but having a body colour of rich copper red, double- or preferably triple-ticked with dark colours. Lack of distinct ticking contrast is a fault. The belly and inside of the legs should be apricot coloured and the tail tip is dark brown. A spine line sometimes extending the length of the tail is allowed. The nose leather and pads should be pink. **Eyes**: colour should be the same as in the brown variety.

Brown Burmese
VARIETY 27
Coat: in maturity the body colour should be a rich, solid, dark seal-brown, shading to a slightly lighter colour on the chest and belly. There should be no white or tabby markings. The latter are permissible but not desirable in kittens. The ears, mask and points should be only very slightly darker than the back coat colour, and in young kittens a somewhat lighter coat colour is usually to be found. **Head**: the face should present a medium wedge and the top of the head should be slightly domed or rounded. In profile, a break at the point where the nose joins the forehead, and a firm chin are required. **Eyes**: large, lustrous, wide apart and slanting towards the nose. The ideal eye colour is intense, golden yellow, but the majority of present-day Burmese of this colour have eyes of chartreuse-yellow. A green tinge in the eye is a fault and intensely green eyes are regarded as being a serious fault. **Ears**: relatively large, wide at the base and slightly rounded at the tip. The

outline of the ear should continue the wedge shape of the face. A jaw pinch is considered a fault. **Tail**: fairly long and slightly tapering, but not whip-like as in the Siamese. The body should be medium in size, elegant and long (but not as long as in the Siamese) and the svelte appearance of the cat is a special consideration.

Blue Burmese
VARIETY 27a
Coat: bluish grey, darker on the back. **Eyes**: large, lustrous, wide apart and slanting towards the nose as in the brown variety. They should be yellow to yellow-green but intensely green eyes must be regarded as being a serious fault.

Chocolate Burmese
VARIETY 27b
This new variety has not as yet been granted championship status. **Coat**: warm, milk chocolate with the ears and mask a shade darker. Evenness of overall colour is highly desirable. The nose leather should be a warm, chocolate-brown but the legs, tail and lower jaw should be the same colour as the back. Young kittens may be faintly barred and the foot pads should be dark pink.

Lilac, Red and Tortie Burmese
VARIETIES 27c, 27d, 27e
These cats have not as yet received championship status but have been granted breed numbers. They differ from the phenotype (the appearance in relation to an accepted standard of points) in colour only.

Havana
VARIETY 29
The Havana is a lithe and sinuous cat, long in the body and of slender proportions. **Coat**: rich, chestnut-brown, quite distinct from that of any other variety. The pads of the feet are pink and the eyes are green. **Head**: a long wedge, narrowing to a fine muzzle. **Eyes**: green, slanting and oriental in shape. **Ears**: large, wide at the base and pricked. Slim legs with dainty, oval paws and a long, whip tail complete this beautiful variety.

Korat
VARIETY 34
This cat has a semi-cobby build with medium bone structure. It has not yet

An outstanding specimen of a female blue-cream Cornish rex showing uniform curling over the entire coat and tail. The broken whiskers are characteristic of both the rex varieties.

achieved championship status. **Coat**: silver-blue. **Head**: heart-shaped face. **Eyes**: green-gold.

Foreign White
VARIETY 35
A delightful variety developed from the Siamese. **Coat**: completely white overall. **Eyes**: blue.

Foreign Lilac
VARIETY 29c
Coat: silvery lavender. **Eyes**: almond shaped. Deep, clear green.

Rex
Both the Cornish and Devon rex cats represent mutations in which the hairs are short and plushy, without guard hairs, and possessed of a distinct curl, wave or ripple, particularly on the back and tail. In both varieties, the whiskers and eyebrows should be crinkled and of good length.

Cornish Rex
VARIETY 33
Head: medium wedge in which the length is about one-third greater than the maximum width, the whole narrowing to a strong chin. The skull should be flat and should extend in a straight line, in profile, to the end of the nose. **Eyes**: oval, of medium size and of a colour consistent with the coat. **Tail**: long, fine and tapering, and covered in curly fur. The body is hard and muscular, slender and of medium length, with long,

Above A well-marked tortoiseshell-and-white shorthair.
Left An odd-eyed white manx. Odd-eyed whites are useful for breeding purposes, as they produce normal-eyed cats of both colours. Taillessness must be absolute.
Right A majestic champion British spotted tabby. In this variety spotting is the most important consideration; the spots must be clear and distinct from the ground colour. In this specimen they are uniform and round.

straight legs terminating in dainty, oval paws.

Devon Rex
VARIETY 33a
The type of the Devon rex is far more extreme than that of the Cornish rex. **Coat**: all colours except bicolours are acceptable. Any white markings other than in tortoiseshell-and-white cats are considered a fault. **Head**: a short wedge, the face full cheeked and terminating in a short muzzle with a most pronounced whisker break, and a nose with a very strongly marked stop. The forehead curves back to a flat skull. **Eyes**: widely set, large, oval-shaped and sloping towards the outer edges of the ears. The eye colour must be in keeping with that of the coat. **Ears**: very large indeed, set rather low, very wide at the base and tapering to rounded tips. The whole ear is covered in fine fur with or without ear muffs. **Tail**: long, tapering and covered with fine, curled fur.

The body is hard and muscular, on the small side and very broad in the chest, with the hindlegs longer than the forelegs. Originally, hairlessness tended to occur in this variety, particularly on the belly. This serious fault has largely been overcome because the judges penalized it severely. The Devon rex is quite different from any other cat in appearance and people either adore it or dislike it intensely. An interesting feature about rex cats is that the two varieties yield straighthaired progeny when mated together, proving that different genes are responsible for the rexing of each variety. Any variety of cat, even the long-hairs, may be rexed by suitable breeding techniques, but to produce longhaired rex varieties is considered by many to be virtually criminal, for the longhair, if rexed, would be almost impossible to keep groomed and the cat could soon be in a hopelessly matted state. The Governing Council of the Cat Fancy has let it be known that it would take a very poor view of anyone attempting such breeding. Siamese cats have been successfully rexed and although many breeders are against this practice the 'si-rex', as these varieties are sometimes called, can be most attractive.

Siamese
All the colour varieties of Siamese must conform to a well-defined standard and although there are some minor differences between them other than colour, it is enough to regard all of them as conforming to the same standard as set down below.

The body must be of medium size, long and svelte. The legs must be proportionately slim with the hindlegs higher than the forelegs; the feet must be small and oval. The body, head, feet, legs and tail must all be in proportion, giving the animal a graceful and well-balanced appearance. **Coat**: very short, fine in texture, glossy and close lying. **Head**: long and well proportioned, with width between the eyes, narrowing in perfectly straight lines to a fine muzzle with a straight profile, strong chin and level bite. **Eyes**: clear blue with a depth of colour appropriate to the colour variety; oriental in shape and slanting towards the nose. No tendency to squint. **Ears**: rather larged and pricked, wide at the base. **Tail**: long, tapering and free from kinks, although a very slight kink at the extremity is allowed.

Seal-pointed Siamese
VARIETY 24
Coat: body colour cream, shading gradually into pale, warm fawn on the back. Kittens paler in colour. **Points**: mask, ears, legs, feet and tail dense and clearly defined seal brown. Mask complete and (except in kittens) connected by tracings with the ears.

Blue-pointed Siamese
VARIETY 24a
Coat: body colour glacial-white, shading gradually to blue on the back, having the same cold tone as the points but of a lighter shade. **Points**: blue; the ears, mask, paws and tail to be of the same colour. The ears must not be darker than the other points. **Eyes**: clear, bright, vivid blue.

Chocolate-pointed Siamese
VARIETY 24b
Coat: body colour ivory all over. Shading, if at all evident, to be the colour of the points but of a lighter shade. In kittens the mask and the front paws tend to develop their colour somewhat slowly. **Points**: milk chocolate; ears, mask, legs, paws and tail to be the same colour. The ears should not be darker than the other points. **Eyes**: clear, bright, vivid blue.

Lilac-pointed Siamese
VARIETY 24c
Coat: body colour off-white or magnolia with shading (if present) to tone with points. **Points:** pinkish grey. Nose leather and pads faded lilac. **Eyes:** clear, light, vivid blue. Blue points are a fault.

Tabby-pointed Siamese
VARIETY 32
Coat: body colour pale, preferably free from body markings and conforming to the general Siamese standard for the particular colour of points. **Points:** seal, blue, chocolate or lilac; an additional variety with tortoiseshell colour points also exists. The mask must have clearly defined stripes, especially around the eyes and nose. Distinct markings on cheeks and darkly spotted whisker pads should be present. Nose leather pink or conforming to the points colour. **Eyes:** brilliant, clear blue; the lids to be dark-rimmed and toning with the points. **Ears:** solid, no stripes. Thumbmarks should be present except in the tortie tabby-points, whose ears should be mottled

A female shell cameo. As yet unrecognized by the Governing Council of the Cat Fancy, the cameos possess a delicate and ethereal beauty which will guarantee their popularity.

Foreign shorthaired varieties are generally more slender and dainty than the British shorthairs. *Left* An Abyssinian. A red variety also exists. *Below* The svelte coat of the Russian blue must possess a silvery sheen, and for true perfection the ears should be close together.

Above These brown (left) and blue Burmese are excellent examples of their respective varieties.
Right A fine cream Burmese, showing a good nose dip.

red and/or cream as in the tortie-pointed Siamese. **Legs:** varied stripes with solid markings on the back of the hindlegs. **Tail:** clearly defined rings of appropriate points colour ending in a solid tip of the same colour. Pads in tortie tabby-points mottled.

Red-pointed Siamese
VARIETY 32a
Coat: white, shading to apricot on the back. Kittens paler. **Points:** mask bright, reddish gold. Nose leather pink. Legs, feet and tail bright, reddish gold. **Eyes:** bright, vivid blue. **Ears:** bright, reddish gold.

Tortie-pointed Siamese
VARIETY 32b
Coat: black or any of its dilutions, i.e. seal, chocolate, blue or lilac, together with red or cream and, sometimes, with both red and cream. Distribution of colour as in other sub-varieties. Barring and ticking is considered a fault. The colours should be well broken with no large patches of any single colour.

SEMI-LONGHAIRED CATS
The following varieties are technically grouped with the longhairs but have a shorter coat and quite distinct type variations.

Turkish
VARIETY 13d
Coat: chalk-white with no trace of yellow. Auburn markings on face with a white blaze. Fur fairly long, soft and silky to the roots with a woolly undercoat. **Head:** short wedge with long nose. **Eyes:** round, light amber with pink-skinned rims. **Ears:** well feathered, large, upright and set close together. **Body:** long but sturdy. Males should be particularly muscular on neck and shoulders. **Legs:** medium length with neat, round feet and well-tufted toes. **Tail:** full, medium length, auburn with faint auburn rings. In kittens the rings are more distinct.

Several shorthair cats, including the Siamese, are often willing to go into water but the Turkish cats are the only ones which readily swim both in the sea and in fresh water. They are also known in some parts of the world as van cats. Some Turkish cats have small auburn markings irregularly placed but this should not necessarily disqualify an otherwise excellent specimen.

Birman
VARIETY 13c
Coat: seal or blue, but the face, tail and paws are dark brown except where white stockings occur in the seals or blue-grey in the blues. The white gloves or stockings are characteristic of the Birmans. Fur should be long with a full ruff. **Head:** wide, round and strongly contoured, with full cheeks. **Eyes:** bright, china blue. **Body:** long but low on the legs. Short, strong paws each with white stockings which run up the back of the hindlegs to an equal distance. **Tail:** fair length, bushy.

OTHER VARIETIES OF CATS
In Europe the various Cat Fancies accept the British standards of points, the only additional variety being the chartreux, which differs very slightly in colour from the British blue shorthair. The American Fancies recognize several additional varieties such as the cameo, the Maine coon, the peke-face, the shaded silver, the Balinese, the American wirehair, the Egyptian mau, the sphynx and the Japanese bobtail. Many of these varieties are extremely attractive and may in time be recognized in Britain, if they are imported in sufficient numbers. The American wirehair is a mutation similar to the rex but a different type of gene is responsible for the wire-like appearance of the coat. These cats are not always recognized by all the American clubs. Shaded silvers are a longhaired variety rather similar to the chinchilla but generally of more robust character. Many British breeders are urging the Council to grant them recognition in order to improve the stamina of British chinchillas. It is also possible to breed blue chinchillas, blue being a Maltese dilution of black.

The above list should enable the would-be cat owner to decide upon the variety of cat which appeals most. It is, of course, virtually impossible to convey the true appearance of a cat by means of verbal description, however well worded, and would-be buyers are advised to visit one of the forty or so shows which are held annually in Britain or the even greater number held on the Continent and in the United States. At a cat show, the cat lover will see every recognized variety of cat and will be able to make a choice far more easily. Moreover, it is possible to talk to breeders and to exhibitors and to obtain a wealth of information which will help you decide upon a suitable variety to purchase. There are always thousands of cat breeders in every major part of the western world who advertise kittens for sale. Not all of these breeders are persons of repute, however, and the prospective buyer is advised not to buy a kitten other than from breeders of high standing. It is difficult for a novice to know with certainty which breeders may be relied upon but the best way to overcome this difficulty is to go to big cat shows and to ask the show manager or one of the judges there to be introduced to a well-known breeder of the variety one likes. In this way, much heartbreak can be avoided and you may be sure that the kitten you buy is in good health and of acceptable show quality, something you can never be sure of when buying from an unknown breeder.

The variety of cat you buy will often depend upon your own nature and attitude to life. Generally speaking, people who prefer longhairs are quite different in character and in emotional make-up from those who buy Siamese; and they, again, are quite different from the shorthair lovers. It is to be supposed that like is reflected in like, and the remarkable energy and intelligence of the Siamese, together with their loud voice and extravert nature makes them less acceptable to people who are themselves somewhat shy and retiring. To be truly happy with the cat you buy it is advisable to examine several varieties 'in the flesh' before making the final choice. It is important to bear in mind that although all cats need grooming, the longhairs need far more regular grooming than the shorthair varieties. It follows, therefore, that the longhairs may prove a little too much of a burden to people of limited free time. On the other hand, longhaired cats possess a most appealing beauty and are far less likely to run up the curtains and generally emulate a whirlwind than are the Siamese and some other related varieties. Another point worth remembering is that Siamese and most of the other shorthaired varieties are good breeders, producing large litters of kittens. The longhaired varieties have become comparatively poor breeders in Britain, largely because of long-term interbreeding result-

ing from the strict quarantine regulations governing the importing of cats into the country. Conversely, the price you are likely to get for kittens of show quality will depend upon the inexorable laws of supply and demand. Longhaired kittens, being comparatively rare at certain times of the year, fetch appreciably higher prices both at home and abroad than the more fertile Siamese and similar varieties.

At this point a word of warning must be given. The successful breeder may have many opportunities to export kittens abroad. It should be borne in mind that not everybody treats cats equally well; some people consider them merely as possessions rather than as sensitive, living creatures. The responsible and compassionate breeder should thus examine the home to which his kitten is to be sent. It is hardly possible to do this when exporting, and the would-be exporter is well advised to seek a reference before launching a kitten along a road which might end in suffering. Finally, before buying a kitten, consider carefully whether you are capable of looking after it properly, both as a kitten and as a grown cat. To live a full and satisfying life a cat must not be imprisoned in a room. It must have fresh air and sunshine, grass and trees and a degree of freedom to live a natural life and to develop the animal grace and perfection with which nature has endowed it. It is unkind to keep a cat if you live in a town flat having no garden. To do so is to subject your pet to an unnatural existence or, alternatively, it means that you must allow it to run in the street. A large balcony can provide only a poor alternative to the freedom of a garden and is not to be recommended in the long term.

Furthermore, a cat loves company, particularly human company. People who live alone and are at work all day should not keep a cat unless they own two or more of them. Remember also that children of a certain age can be terribly cruel to animals without realizing it, so never give kittens, or indeed any other animal, to very young, unsupervised children. Another difficulty is that children often lose interest in an animal after a few weeks or even a few days, and for this reason it is always ill-advised to give kittens as Christmas or birthday presents unless you are certain that they will be cherished and well looked after.

Above Derived from the Siamese, the foreign lilac has a coat possessing a silvery lilac sheen.
Left Devon rex. Of the two common rex varieties, the Devon rex is more extreme in type than the Cornish rex.
Right The Havana, another popular foreign shorthaired cat.

Cat care

BUYING A KITTEN

If you wish to buy a kitten you will have a choice of three sources: the pet shop, the breeder and the cat show. Many pet shops are well run and the animals there are kept in excellent condition. Unfortunately, this cannot be said of all pet shops and it may be difficult for the prospective buyer to ensure that the kitten he or she acquires in this manner is completely healthy. Moreover, if you are seeking a pedigree kitten and have little or no specialist knowledge in the field, you may well purchase an animal which is inferior in genotype or phenotype. The genotype of an animal is its entire, genetical make-up derived from its parents, while the word phenotype refers to the external appearance of the animal in relation to the standard of points approved for the variety.

Admittedly, if you are simply looking for a pet, and if the kitten is healthy, phenotype and genotype may be thought to be of minor importance. Conversely, if you are prepared to pay the price of a thoroughbred animal, then even if you intend to keep it purely as a pet it makes good sense to buy one of high quality. It is surprising how often people who buy pedigree pets later decide to show them or to use them for breeding. If your kitten turns out to be of poor type or badly

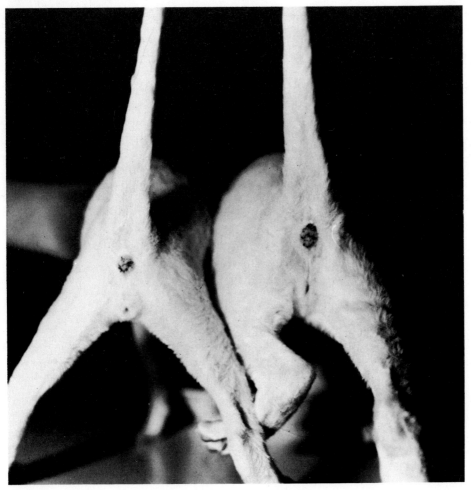

How to sex cats. On the left, a male and on the right, a female. The anus and vulva are close together on the female, and in older male cats the testes can be felt. Remember that males possess rudimentary teats, so their presence should not be used as a discriminatory feature.

bred, you will make a poor start to your career as a cat breeder or exhibitor. In short, if there is the slightest possibility that you may later decide to be more than a pet owner it is best to buy your kitten either from a reputable specialist breeder or at a championship cat show.

You will always find a list of breeders in cat journals and the Editor will be glad to refer the enquirer to the Secretary of a suitable cat club from whom all other information may be obtained. Well-known breeders cannot afford to sell poor kittens, while if buying at a show you will have the advantage of making a choice once the judging is over and the award cards have been put on the pens. If you decide to buy a kitten from a pet shop, the following points may be of assistance in helping you to choose one that is in good health. Healthy kittens are playful and mischievous, and a dull, listless animal should be avoided. Carefully inspect around the eyes for signs of inflammation of the lids, and ensure that the ears are clean and show no sign of the brown dirt which so often denotes ear canker or the presence of ear mites. The fur of a kitten, unless it is too young to sell, should be close lying and glossy in the case of a shorthair, and clean, upstanding and fluffy in a longhair. Make a careful inspection of the coat for signs of fleas or their dirt and examine the anus and the base of the tail for traces of diarrhoea. Feel the weight of the kitten. If it seems very light for its size, or if its backbone is too prominent, do not buy it. Generally, there is something quite unmistakable about a healthy young animal which can be perceived instinctively by the discerning eye. If you doubt your own judgement, take along an experienced friend or buy the kitten conditionally upon the verdict of a veterinary surgeon.

Always ask if the kitten has been inoculated against feline infectious enteritis (F.I.E.) and if you are told that it has, demand a copy of the veterinary certificate of inoculation. If it has not, and you decide to buy the kitten, have it inoculated immediately since this virus disease is a killer.

Introducing kittens into the home

A person buying a kitten may already own one or more cats or dogs, and great care must be taken that resident pets do not attack the new arrival. Adult animals, whether cats or dogs, will seldom seriously attack a very young kitten but exceptions do occur and experienced owners will deal with the situation by making a fuss of the residents rather than of the newcomer. This avoids much of the jealousy which is so often the root of disharmony, and under normal conditions will induce the established pets to accept the kitten very quickly. On the other hand, do not be unduly worried if an older resident appears to be putting the kitten very firmly in its place. It is merely establishing its superiority as it would in the wild. A few days will normally suffice for a young kitten to be accepted fully by older animals. If your other pets turn on the kitten viciously, however, take great care to separate them and only allow them to be together when you are present. During these meetings, take special care to make a great fuss of the older animals to show them that your affection has not been stolen by the newcomer. It is only in the most exceptional cases that this technique will fail to produce the desired result in a matter of days.

Where there are no other animals present these problems will naturally not arise and all the owner need do is to provide the kitten with a sleeping basket placed in a warm corner which is free from draughts, and with a toilet tray readily available (see page 90). Many people allow their pets to sleep on, or even in, their own beds but generally speaking this is not a good practice. Not only is it unhygienic, but a young kitten can be injured if you turn over during sleep. The matter of diet is dealt with elsewhere in this book but always make sure that a plentiful supply of clean water is readily available in every room in which the kitten may be confined.

Should there be any very young children in the house, ensure that they are not allowed to ill-treat the kitten. Children sometimes behave very mischievously with young animals and such a tendency should be firmly discouraged. It is the duty of every adult to teach children to show compassion towards animals. In this context it should be remembered that even in the absence of actual cruelty, excessive handling of a young animal is in itself a form of torment.

Guarding dangerous objects

A very important point to remember is that

Playful and intelligent, the seal-pointed Siamese is the most popular Siamese variety of all.

The points of lilac-pointed Siamese must show no traces of blue.

The true 'Siamese look' is exemplified by this lovely tabby-point.

delightful female blue tortie-pointed Siamese. Blue is just one of several colours in which this variety is available.

young animals are very inquisitive and care must be taken to place guards around fires and other potentially dangerous objects. Do not allow a kitten to play around your feet while you are cooking. You may trip over it and spill the contents of a boiling kettle or saucepan over the unfortunate animal. In particular, make sure that electric cables are not allowed to lie where the kitten might start playing with them. A kitten's teeth are like needles and, if the current is switched on, penetration of the insulation by the teeth would mean instant death. If your kitten shows a tendency to play with electric cables tap it on the nose with a rolled-up newspaper and speak harshly to it when you catch it in the act. It will soon mend its ways.

Toys and scratching posts

All intelligent young animals get bored from time to time. It is when kittens get bored that they tend to claw your furniture. You can avoid this by providing your kitten with a scratching post and a few toys, such as a rabbit's foot hanging by a piece of string.

One leg of your kitchen table with a piece of strong canvas firmly and neatly tied around it will make an ideal scratching post and is to be recommended unless your kitten spends most of its time in the garden, scratching about and climbing trees. Should you decide to buy some of the cat toys available in most pet shops, take care to see that they are soundly made and either too big to swallow or else soft enough throughout to do no harm if torn apart and eaten.

Weaning kittens

The act of suckling is enjoyed both by the kitten and by the mother cat and constitutes one of nature's provisions to ensure the continuance of life by a suitable application both of instinct and of the pleasure-pain sensation. It follows that in many cases, particularly where the litter is a small one, the mother cat will continue to suckle her kittens long after they are perfectly capable of feeding themselves. To frustrate this tendency, kittens should be weaned as soon as they are able to lap from a saucer and certainly by the time they are five to six

Below **Kittens will derive hours of enjoyment as well as exercise from a dangling piece of string, and their antics are a delight to watch.** *Right* **Scratching posts exercise the claws and save your furniture. A piece of sacking or canvas secured around a kitchen table leg will serve the same purpose.**

Left A beautifully
marked Turkish cat.
Turkish cats are willing
and capable swimmers,
an unusual
phenomenon among
cats.
Above A male Maine
coon, a popular
American variety.
Right A female Birman.
Both the Birman and
the Turkish are semi-
longhaired varieties.

Overleaf A full-grown
cat still being suckled
by its mother. This
practice must be
discouraged as it
exhausts the mother.

weeks old. Cow's milk is only half as concentrated as cat's milk, providing less protein and fewer Calories. While at five weeks one can rely on the fact that a kitten fed on cow's milk is free to consume a greater volume than that which it is likely to obtain from its mother, it must be encouraged to take solid foods such as finely minced meat, fish, chicken, liver or egg, beginning with very small quantities and increasing according to appetite. Occasionally, a cat's milk supply will dry up before the kittens are ready for weaning, and feeding by means of a dropper fitted with a thin rubber tube must be carried out as described on page 89 under feeding kittens. Failure to wean kittens at a reasonable age may impose unnecessary strain upon the mother.

In conclusion, the introduction of a kitten into your home should normally be accomplished easily and quickly if care is taken and if an understanding relationship is established. Cats respond rapidly to kind treatment and will amply return their owner's affection.

CAT BASKETS AND COLLARS

A wicker sleeping basket is pleasant to have, but a kitten will be just as happy in a cardboard or wooden box lined with many thicknesses of newspaper which may be burnt and replaced when necessary. This is a matter of choice. However, no home in which there is a cat or kitten should be without a travelling basket complete with a hinged lid retained by straps. Should you ever need to take your kitten or cat on a journey or to the vet this is the only safe way to do it. Carrying baskets can be purchased at cat shows as indeed can all the items you may require. Alternatively, good pet shops generally have an adequate selection of them. When buying a carrying basket remember that your kitten will soon grow into a cat. Buy a basket that is sufficiently large. Some of the modern baskets are made of transparent plastic and are highly recommended, but if you prefer one of the wicker type, wrap brown paper around the four sides (but not the top and bottom) to exclude wind.

Cats which enjoy freedom to play in the garden or go out into the street should be provided with a collar bearing an engraved disc carrying your address or telephone number. It is dangerous to place an ordinary

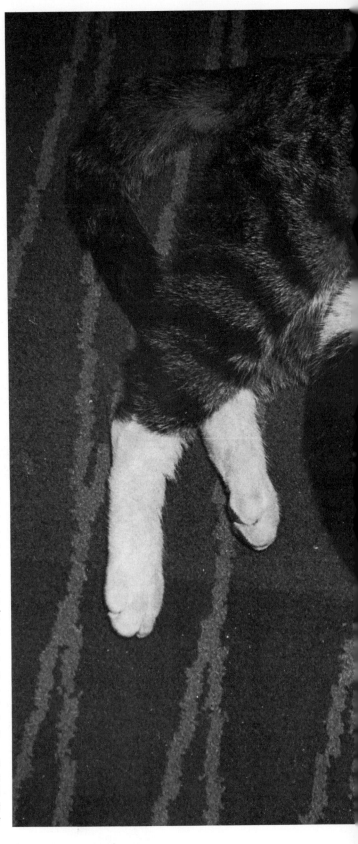

Three varieties which
are recognized by
American Fancies but,
as yet, not by the
Governing Council of
the Cat Fancy are the
bronze mau (left); the
shaded silver (above), a
vigorous variety
intermediate between
the chinchilla and the
smoke; and the
Balinese (right).

leather collar around a cat's neck, however, since such a collar may result in the animal's death if it should become caught by it while climbing trees, etc. The ideal collar has a central section made of thick elastic which will expand under such circumstances and allow the animal to slip its head free. It is far better to lose an occasional collar than to risk your pet's life.

GROOMING AND BATHING

In the author's view (and not all experts are in agreement on this issue) cats should not be bathed unless they have become unusually soiled or, of course, unless they are being especially prepared for a show. Even in the latter case, bathing should only be resorted to if there is a special reason. Shorthaired cats and kittens living in natural surroundings require little more than grooming with a fine comb, particularly during the period of advanced moult. Cats are extremely fastidious animals and

anyone who has observed the care with which a cat will lick every part of its fur will soon realize that little more than plenty of hand grooming is needed. Because cats live in artificial light in the home the moult, which in nature occurs annually as the days lengthen, may persist, to some degree, throughout the year. In shorthairs, the loose hairs and dead hair follicles are most easily removed by combing with a very fine steel comb and then grooming with the hand or with a piece of chamois leather. Nevertheless, cats may come home covered in paint, tar or some other persistent substance. In such cases bathing, together with other specific treatments, may on occasion be necessary.

Longhaired cats require combing and brushing far more frequently than shorthairs, and failure to carry out these duties daily may result in the formation of fur balls in the cat's stomach. Also, longhaired cats are more likely to pick up dirt from streets

These baskets are of excellent design but are not draught-proof, therefore they should be kept in a warm corner. Newspaper is a useful bedding material as it can easily be replaced when soiled.

A hinged travelling basket. Brown paper or polythene wrapped round the sides will prevent draughts. Do not cover the top or bottom, however.

and fields, in which case a good bath is often the only solution to an otherwise unsavoury situation. Bathing must be carried out in a warm, draught-free room using lukewarm, preferably soft water. Mild detergents may be used but a good quality soap powder is preferable. The cat must be rinsed thoroughly in several changes of water and then dried with a thick towel, or with a hair dryer if the cat is not afraid of it. Once dry, the coat should be thoroughly combed and brushed. A little talcum powder sprinkled into the coat is very helpful in the final grooming. A greasy coat is best dry cleaned using warm bran, as described on page 100. Most cats do not object to dry cleaning and all prefer it to being bathed.

CLEANING EARS, EYES AND TEETH

In a perfectly healthy cat living in ideal surroundings there should be little need to clean the ears, which are so constructed that in health the cat can keep them perfectly clean by itself. If the inner ear flap does tend to become a little soiled, a wipe with a cloth moistened with olive oil is all that is required. Occasionally, the owner's attention may be drawn to an ear condition by seeing the cat scratching at its ear flap; if

A tabby-pointed
Siamese and her litter.

Left Three appealing
seven-week-old
Siamese kittens.
Right Part of a modern
well-run cattery. The
houses and large runs
are spaced apart to
minimize the risk of
infection.

nothing is visible externally a few drops of olive oil may be introduced into the ear with a dropper. A thorough, external massage will generally loosen the wax causing the discomfort, and very soon the cat's ear will be back to normal. If this treatment fails to yield results, let the cat be examined by a veterinary surgeon. On no account should you probe the cat's ear with any instrument as permanent damage may be brought about. Should an ear become encrusted with a brown or grey discharge or with a waxy or resinous deposit, once again the veterinary surgeon must be consulted as the cat may be suffering from canker caused by an ear mite infestation. Both of these conditions are easily cured by professional treatment. It is appreciated that veterinary services can be costly and cat owners sometimes try to treat apparently simple disorders themselves. If the home treatment does not work quickly, however, seek professional help at once. An excessive delay may convert an acute but easily curable condition into a chronic and resistant one. If you are short of money there are many veterinary organizations available who show great kindness and understanding and leave it to the pet owners to pay what they can. Thus there is no real excuse for anyone failing to provide veterinary treatment when a cat requires it.

In some of the strongly typed longhairs the tear ducts tend to be compressed, with the result that the eyes are more or less constantly weeping and unless frequent and regular attention is given the eyelids may become infected and inflamed. Conversely, cats of normal nose structure very seldom suffer from dirty eyes and if the lids do become inflamed a serious infection or a dietary imbalance must be suspected. If the condition does not respond rapidly to treatment with eye drops or boracic acid solution, a veterinary surgeon should be consulted.

The teeth of a healthy cat should never need cleaning providing it is properly fed on a suitably balanced diet. If the gums become red or inflamed it is often a sign that the cat is suffering either from an excess or a deficiency of vitamin A.

CUTTING CLAWS

A cat which spends much of its time out of doors indulging in cat-like activities such as climbing trees will keep its claws neatly trimmed. On the other hand, the claws of a cat constrained to live much of its time indoors will tend to grow too long and the owner will have to attend to them from time to time. A pair of good side-cutters is the best instrument to use, and only the transparent tip of the nail should be cut off. This simple task is best carried out with the cat lying in your lap. A thumb in the ball of the cat's paw and the forefingers of the hand retracting the sheath exposes the nail and enables the cut to be made quickly and neatly. Under no circumstances must a cat be declawed except for surgical reasons, and then it must be entrusted to a veterinary surgeon. Failure to trim a cat's claws may result in the cat trying to perform the task itself with the help of its teeth.

SHOULD CATS BE PUT OUT AT NIGHT?

Putting cats out at night, particularly in cold and inclement weather, is a practice which should be avoided. A well-designed trap door through which a cat may leave or enter the house at will is a sensible and kindly provision, however. Cats may occasionally suffer a stomach disorder and such a trap would allow the cat to go outside to perform its toilet and then return at will. Well-designed trap doors may be bought at most

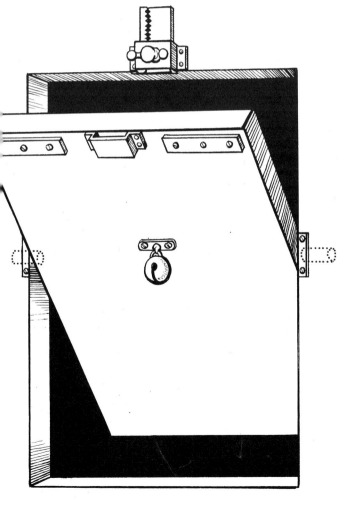

n excellent design of
t flap which can be
cked shut when
sired.

of the major cat shows or may easily be made at home. Refinements include draught-excluding devices and internal bolts.

SIMPLE FIRST AID

Veterinary matters are fully considered in another section of this book but there are one or two situations in which the cat owner, faced with the problem of how to handle an injured cat, may take the wrong action unless he has an elementary knowledge of how to restrain a frightened cat or deal with a pressing emergency. A cat badly hurt in an accident is likely to be either very violent or else in a state of severe shock. This condition may be brought about by any kind of serious injury be it a wound, a burn or internal damage caused by a passing motor vehicle. In shock, a cat will appear prostrate and dazed and sometimes the depression may be so severe as to cause complete immobility, while at other times the cat may exhibit considerable excitement. In most cases of shock the body temperature can fall very rapidly to a dangerously low level. In some respects, the phenomenon of shock is the outward evidence of a reflex defence mechanism involving the release of a series of complex chemical substances into the bloodstream. Histamine is one such substance. It is released by certain types of cell and has the effect of causing a rapid dilation of blood vessels, with the result that the blood pressure in the main circulatory system falls, often to the degree that unconsciousness occurs. It is feasible that but for the occurrence of this phenomenon in the wild an injured cat might have exposed itself to enemies when it was in no condition to offer adequate resistance.

The best treatment for shock is to cover the cat with warm blankets and to administer a fluid such as glucose saline by means of a spoon or dropper. Care must be taken to ensure that the liquid is given slowly enough not to choke the animal. In cases where the cat behaves violently, it is first necessary to restrain it. This may normally be accomplished by grasping it firmly by the loose skin at the back of the neck and lifting it wholly or partly off the ground. Held in this position a cat tends to curl up into a more or less foetal position and simply hangs limply, as a kitten hangs from its mother's mouth. It may then easily be wrapped up in a blanket in preparation for the next step, which is to take it to a veterinary surgeon with the least loss of time.

If your cat has suffered a wound which is bleeding, you should do nothing about it unless the bleeding is severe. In the event of slight or even moderate bleeding the cat can usually accomplish more with its tongue than you can with bandages and salves. In the event of very severe bleeding, however, where it appears that an artery has been cut, pressure should be applied against the artery at a close point between the wound and the heart. Alternatively, where the position of the wound makes this possible, a tourniquet should be applied to stop the bleeding. It is very important to loosen the tourniquet every ten minutes.

If the cat has swallowed a noxious substance

A cat's feet, or even its coat, may be contaminated by noxious substances such as paint, paraffin (kerosene) or horticultural sprays that have been inadvertently spilt. The cat's remedy is to 'wash' and so the noxious substance is swallowed and further absorbed. The owner should therefore try to remove the substance as soon as possible and, in the main, common sense measures are effective. Thus any water-soluble substance should be washed off with soap or mild detergent and then rinsed clean. Tar, thick motor oil or other oil-soluble substances, should be rubbed with butter and wiped off with paper tissues before a final wash in soap or mild detergent is given. Most horticultural sprays are water soluble and will respond to washing with soap and water, but it is worth remembering that certain insecticides are far more dangerous when in an oily base as they may be very rapidly absorbed through the skin, and the butter method should not be employed.

Cats rarely suffer from ingested poisons as most are particular in their choice of food. The exception is in the case of slug bait, particularly slug bait which has been mixed with some substance such as meal.

Cats that have eaten slug pellets usually show marked hypersensitivity to all stimuli – sound, touch and light. The animal should be placed in a quiet, dark room and a veterinary surgeon contacted for advice. In all such cases, a sample of the substance ingested or, better still, the tin or bottle from which it came is of help to the veterinary surgeon in assessing the best treatment.

Cats seldom eat mice and rats that have been poisoned with rat bait, although it is worth mentioning that the modern 'safe' rat baits are not quite as safe as their makers suggest.

RABIES AND THE QUARANTINE LAWS

Rabies is a virus disease capable of affecting many warm-blooded animals including man, cat and dog. It is usually transmitted in the saliva from the bite of a rabid animal, the virus then invading the nerve tissue and leading to a particularly horrible death after a variable period of a few days to six months. Once the disease is in a country it infects the wildlife and is difficult or impossible to eradicate. In Europe the main carriers of the disease are foxes and these, coming into the suburbs at night to scavenge, meet domestic cats and so introduce rabies into the domestic cat population. In Central and South America the vampire bat is the most important carrier and many cattle thus become infected, whilst in the United States skunks, foxes and raccoons are commonly implicated.

Those countries that are free of the disease, notably Britain, Australia and New Zealand, impose strict quarantine regulations on all dogs and cats entering their countries. In Britain cats (as well as other mammals) undergo quarantine for six months, wherever they come from, whilst no dog or cat is allowed into Australia or New Zealand unless it has been in Britain for twelve months; in other words, a cat going from the United States must come to Britain and undergo six months quarantine and a further six months at large in the country, before permission to proceed to Australia or New Zealand can be obtained. Some other countries, mainly in northern Europe where rabies is rare, restrict importations or impose lesser quarantine periods, so that it is essential that any cat owner should obtain details of individual countries' regulations on this matter before proceeding to emigrate. Many countries insist on anti-rabies inoculations and although until recently they were considered unsafe for cats, new vaccines have proved absolutely safe.

Nutrition and feeding

Most domestic cats which have access to gardens and fields go hunting despite regular feeding by human beings, and a good mother cat will always teach her kittens to fend for themselves. In the absence of such maternal tuition a domestic, town-reared cat is unable to maintain itself except by scavenging. This accounts for the poor appearance of town strays which will always attempt to reassociate themselves with human 'meal-tickets' at the earliest opportunity.

Feeding your cat raises a number of important questions. Firstly, what particular food constituents does a healthy cat require. Are some of these more important than others and do needs vary with age? Secondly, how much food should a cat receive and how often should it be fed?

Thirdly, what foods are available for feeding cats, how far do these go in meeting their needs and are there any special problems associated with feeding fresh or manufactured foods? The following pages answer these questions.

FOOD CONSTITUENTS REQUIRED BY CATS

The carcass of a small rodent (one of the cat's natural food sources) consists of the following: water 70 percent; protein 14 percent; fat 10 percent; carbohydrate 1 percent; minerals 1 percent; vitamins are supplied by the prey's liver, and calcium and other salts are supplied by the prey's bones. These proportions can be considered to make up the ideal diet for an adult cat. Therefore the food that you feed your cat

This predatory cat has caught its own food – a mouse. Although hairy skin is usually rejected by vomiting, the rest of the prey provides all the nutritional requirements of the cat, particularly protein from the prey's muscle, calcium salts from its bone and vitamin A from its liver.

should supply it with proteins, fats, carbohydrates, vitamins, mineral salts and water. The problems which arise in feeding cats result mainly from their very strict adaptation to a carnivorous diet, for they have lost to a large extent the capacity to digest or utilize coarse plant materials. They have become adapted to eating relatively large amounts of meat protein for their size (this is normally 30 percent to 50 percent of the dry weight of the diet). Cats cannot exist on a low protein diet in the same way that human beings can but they can survive very well on diets rich in fat, providing there is plenty of protein with it, as is the case with cheap cuts of meat. Although some cats rather like sugar, sucrose (table sugar) is damaging and lactose (milk sugar) is poorly digested and not absorbed and can therefore cause severe digestive disturbance leading to diarrhoea. The only form of carbohydrate which cats can digest readily is cooked starch (as in bread), biscuits and boiled potatoes; in fact there is very little carbohydrate in the normal diet of a wild cat. Attempts have been made to replace meat proteins by vegetable or synthetic protein in order to reduce the high cost of the protein diet needed by cats, but these have not been very successful. Some people suggest that this is because vegetable protein does not have the same amino acid pattern as meat, but it is difficult to say whether this is important or not because we do not yet know the precise amino acid requirements of the cat.

While fats and carbohydrates are completely utilized in the body and form carbon dioxide and water, proteins form additional nitrogenous waste products such as urea and creatinine. These have to be expelled dissolved in water and are thus excreted by the kidneys in the urine. The kidneys have to work much harder in the cat than in a dog or human, since cats eat twice or three times as much protein as a dog, and four or five times as much as a man in relation to their weight.

Cats have an exceptionally high requirement of vitamin A (retinol). This is necessary to keep cell membranes in working order and is used in the light-sensing mechanism in the retina of the eye. Vitamin E (tocopherol) is also important to cats but kittens need very much less antirachitic vitamin D (cholecalciferol) than puppies or even human babies, as they seem to be able to manufacture it in their skins under the influence of sunlight. Kittens brought up in dark conditions until they are four to five months old tend to suffer from rickets or osteoporosis (weakened bones) but the most usual cause of this condition is lack of sufficient calcium in the diet. In the wild, cats eat the whole carcasses of small birds and rodents including the liver and bones. From the former they get supplies of vitamins and from the latter calcium and phosphorus in the correct ratio (about 1:1) for bone growth and replacement. When domestic cats are fed meat alone they are deprived of both vitamins and mineral salts, and kittens especially show severe deficiency signs such as fractured and deformed bones, usually at four to six months of age. Kittens and cats need the B vitamin thiamin, to maintain normal activity of the nerves and the central nervous system – this vitamin is easily destroyed by cooking and canned diets should contain additional thiamin to make up for the loss in processing. B vitamins (riboflavin, niacin and biotin) are usually plentiful in the normal diet and deficiency is only seen in sick cats, particularly those suffering from virus infections. Healthy cats can manufacture their own vitamin C and therefore do not normally need this in their food. A vitamin called folic acid can be inadequate in diets made up mainly of cooked meat. Cats which have access to fresh, young grass – which they are usually very fond of – will always receive plenty of folic acid, however.

Like other animals, cats need sodium and potassium in their food to make good daily losses in urine. These minerals are called *electrolytes* and are of great importance in keeping the fluid systems of the body functioning properly. They are rapidly lost when the cat has severe diarrhoea or constantly vomits. In such circumstances your vet should inject water containing sodium and potassium salts directly into the body either under the skin or into a vein. Normally there is plenty of sodium and potassium in the ordinary diet of a healthy cat. The need for calcium and phosphorus in a balanced form has already been mentioned, especially for kittens and pregnant and lactating mother cats. Small amounts of these are needed to maintain the health of all the other cells in the body, including bone which acts as a storehouse, and are present at a constant level in blood. Very small amounts of a number of other minerals are needed including iron for haemoglobin in the blood, iodine for manufacturing the hormone thyroxin in the thyroid gland and copper, zinc, manganese, magnesium and cobalt for forming complex enzymes which regulate the metabolism of cells. With the possible exception of iodine, these are seldom deficient in the diet. Iodine is best provided by an occasional meal of sea fish. Adult cats need no additional iron in their diet unless they have become anaemic due to excessive loss of blood from an accident, while kittening or as a result of attack by blood parasites. Many of these metallic substances are highly toxic when given in excessive amounts, hence the great danger of daily mineral and vitamin supplements to food. Unless specially recommended by the vet for a sick, convalescent or pregnant cat or for a growing kitten, supplements should be avoided and confidence placed in a good, mixed diet to supply the vitamins and mineral salts needed.

HOW MUCH FOOD SHOULD A CAT HAVE AND HOW OFTEN SHOULD IT BE FED?

In a cat's body, protein, fats and carbohydrates undergo a controlled process of burning called *oxidation* which releases energy. This energy is measured as heat in units called Calories. The energy value of individual food constituents and the daily energy output of the cat have both been measured, and can thus be compared. When the cat's food provides about the same number of Calories that its body is using, then the cat's weight remains stationary. If, however, there are more Calories in the food than are being used up, then the excess food will be stored as protein and fat and the cat will gain weight. On the other hand, if the cat receives too few Calories from its food it will draw on some of its reserve fat and protein to make up the deficit and will lose weight. Regular weighing (the kitchen scales can be used) will give a useful guide to correct feeding; most people tend to overfeed adult cats and an occasional weight check will help to prevent this. Kittens on the other hand need more Calories in relation to their body weight (see table), partly because they are growing very rapidly but also because small animals have a relatively greater surface area exposed to the cooling effects of the environment and therefore need more food to make up for heat loss.

In the wild state adult cats do not necessarily make a kill every day, and under domestic conditions feeding once daily is probably sufficient. Some owners like to give a small meal such as milk at breakfast time. There is no harm in this provided that an allowance is made for breakfast or snacks in measuring out the main meal.

Daily food requirements of cats according to age

| Age | Expected body wt | | Daily ration | |
---	lb	kg	oz	g
Newborn	0·25	0·12	1·0	30
5 weeks	1·0	0·5	3·0	85
10 weeks	2·0	1·0	5·0	140
20 weeks	4·5	2·0	6·0	170
30 weeks	6·5	3·0	7·0	200
Adult ♂	10·0	4·5	8·5	240
Adult ♀ (pregnant)	7·5	3·5	8·5	240
Adult ♀ (lactating)	5·5	2·5	14·0	415
Neuter ♂	9·0	4·0	7·0	200
Neuter ♀	5·5	2·5	5·0	140

The table gives some guidance as to how much food you should give your cat during the various stages of development. For kittens the calculations are based on cat's milk and for older cats on an 'ideal' diet as described earlier.

Very fat, overfed cats are, like human beings, more prone to disease and early death than active, lithe, correctly fed cats. Young kittens, or mother cats feeding kittens, need to be fed twice or three times a day.

On the whole, cats are more fussy in their eating habits than are dogs. They are rather easily put off when feeding, especially by strange noises and strong lights and also by strange people or animals, even other cats. They are also sensitive to the kind of container the food is in; it should be either disposable or regularly washed (away from human dishes) and thoroughly rinsed with plenty of water to remove any smell of washing-up liquid or disinfectant. Cats choose their food by smell and also by consistency; the food should be neither too hard nor too soft. Most, but not all cats, enjoy milk or tea but fresh water must always be available although cats often develop a characteristic habit of lapping water from a favourite tap, sink or pond. Insufficient supplies of drinking water may result in the formation of a very concentrated urine, followed by blockage of the urinary tract in some male cats.

SUITABLE FOODS FOR CATS

The range of foodstuffs available to domestic cats falls into several broad categories; raw, home-prepared foods; cooked and processed foods intended for other animals such as dogs and human beings; and processed foods made specially for cats by pet food manufacturers.

Raw foods suitable for cats include all types of butcher's meat, and offal such as liver; poultry and poultry trimmings; surplus or infertile eggs; rabbits and freshly killed day-old chicks; and small rodents, birds and frogs which they catch for themselves. These foods are a good source of protein and fat, and most closely resemble natural food. Provided the diet is varied and *not* confined to carcass meat, cats remain extremely healthy on these foods. They are,

A daily feeding programme for your cat (¾-full grown)

MORNING SNACK (Optional)	½ teacup of cow's milk, with a teaspoonful of codliver oil stirred in twice a week. Dried or diluted, unsweetened, condensed milk can also be used. Goat's milk can be used instead of cow's milk.
EVENING MEAL (To be given at a regular time)	Portion of canned or fresh food (containing 75 percent moisture). 6–9oz (170–250g) is equivalent to 2–3 level teacups. Adjust the quantity according to the size, age and activity of the cat. A varied diet is important and the following alternatives can be offered. Small tin of meat-based, canned cat food.
or	Portion of *fresh* white fish, herring, mackerel or fish pieces. Cook lightly and serve *with* bones and juices.
or	4–6oz (96–170g) liver, preferably raw. Serve with biscuit meal or dry cat food.
or	Small tin of fish-based cat food.
or	Minced or chopped fresh or deep-frozen meat. Thaw before serving.
or	Chicken pieces (with bones) or small tin of chicken-based food.
or	Portion of rabbit. Cook lightly and serve with bones.
or	½ teacup of dry cat food with beaten egg poured over.
or	Meat or fish plate scraps or cooking trimmings when available in sufficient quantity. Must be fresh.

The evening meal can be supplemented with small quantities of cooked potato, brown bread soaked in gravy, well-cooked vegetables, puppy meal, etc., according to the tastes of the cat. The cat should not be allowed to gain excess weight once fully grown. A teaspoonful of cod-liver oil should be given twice weekly.

of course, expensive unless you have access to a special source, such as a poultry farm, in the immediate neighbourhood. There are two dangers associated with these foods. Firstly, they are easily contaminated with micro-organisms which cause food spoilage and are capable of infecting your pet. Secondly, a cat can become addicted to a particular food (for instance carcass meat, chicken or liver) and disastrous consequences can develop if it refuses to eat anything else. In addition carcass meat is deficient in calcium, iodine and vitamin A, resulting in osteoporosis (loss of bone substance) and infertility. Liver on the other hand is highly nutritious – so much so that adult cats eating nothing but liver produce new bony outgrowths around their joints so that movement becomes very difficult and the cat becomes rigid. This is due to an excess of vitamin A, and the same effect is the result of giving excessive and continuous doses of fish liver oils and pharmaceutical vitamin A. The stiffness slowly improves when the source of vitamin A is removed from the diet.

Fresh milk is a very acceptable food to most cats and supplies protein, calcium and riboflavin but many adult cats are unable to digest milk sugar (lactose). They have persistent diarrhoea, sometimes very severe, when given either liquid or dried milk in any form. In some cases the condition is due to an allergic reaction to the protein in cow's milk. Goat's milk is a satisfactory non-allergic substitute for cow's milk.

The raw foods listed above, with the addition of fish, can be prepared and cooked in the home. Although destroying micro-organisms and softening the food, prolonged or excessive boiling will result in a loss of palatability and the destruction of heat-sensitive vitamins such as thiamin.

Cooked and processed foods include plate scraps and dog foods. Cats will eat the remains of stews and meat scraps and these can form up to one-third of the daily food supply without harm, and will certainly reduce costs. Dog foods based on meat, offal or chicken are accepted by some cats but on the whole they are less acceptable than products made specially for cats.

Foods manufactured for cats are usually either canned or dried. Frozen foods, or the newer soft-moist foods, are sometimes available and the frozen foods especially are acceptable, but expensive. Many claim to be 'complete' foods, in other words no other kind of food is needed. Such claims should be treated with reservations and from early kittenhood the cat should be encouraged to eat a variety of different foods. This prevents addiction to a particular diet – once this has developed it is extremely hard to break – and, furthermore, a deficiency in one food may be compensated for by another food in a mixed diet. Tinned foods with a water content of 70–80 percent are probably best for the cat since their composition is closer to natural foods. Canned cat food is made up of a mixture of minced or chunky ingredients, usually including a variety of meats, offal, poultry and fish, with a small proportion of fat and usually a considerable quantity of carbohydrate (cooked starch). A declaration of constituents on the can label is mandatory in the United States and also in many continental countries, and will probably soon become obligatory in Britain. All ingredients must be in a perfectly wholesome condition before processing because cats can easily detect the odour of unfresh food and will refuse to eat it. It is then cut up or minced, mixed with vitamins, minerals, liver powder and colouring, cooked and while still hot poured into cans which are immediately sealed and sterilized. Both the time and the temperature of the sterilization process are critical – if the time is too brief and the temperature too low it will fail to destroy the micro-organisms and, conversely, excesses of time and temperature will destroy vitamins and alter proteins so that they become indigestible. Canned cat foods often have a rather limited shelf life and should be used before they are six months old. They are usually stamped with a date and batch code number which should be quoted in any correspondence or enquiry concerning the food.

Dried cat foods are made of similar materials to canned foods although they sometimes contain more carbohydrates. The mix is rapidly dried in hot air to form a light, biscuit-like material. This is cheaper to package and lighter to transport, although it occupies more space. Dry diets have been carefully developed by manufacturers so that they are now very acceptable to most cats although if used continuously they may result in the cat's consuming much less liquid each day. The same amount of waste products are produced as in a moist diet, so that the urine becomes very concentrated. Some of the waste products then form crystals which may block narrow passages in the urinary tract of male cats (uro-lithiasis). This is potentially dangerous for tom cats some of which – possibly one in ten of the male cat population – are particularly susceptible to these blockages, a condition requiring immediate veterinary attention (see p. 115). To avoid such complaints dried cat foods, if used regularly, should be fed mixed with warm water. Dry food can also be given occasionally to help keep the gums healthy and the teeth clean and free from tartar. Small bones, preferably raw, also serve this purpose and in addition help to provide calcium. Generally speaking, you should not leave a bowl of dry food available all day, especially if the cat is shut into a flat or cattery. Regular meals given once or twice daily are much more satisfactory.

Composition of different types of food for cats

	Approx percentage moisture	Approx percentage dry solids
Fresh meat	70	30
Fresh fish	80	20
Processed canned food	75	25
Soft-moist manufactured food	25	75
Processed dried food	10	90

Note the differences in the amount of water available in the cat's food, also the larger percentage of solids present in dried food. Therefore you need only feed one-third as much dried food by weight as fresh food.

FEEDING KITTENS

Feeding routine for hand-reared kittens

Age (weeks post-partum)	Feed	Number of meals in 24 hrs	Volume of milk per meal		Expected body weight	
			teaspoon	ml	oz	g
1	Milk mixture in bottle	12–9	$\frac{1}{2}$–$1\frac{1}{2}$	2–7	$3\frac{1}{2}$–7	100–200
2	,, ,, ,, ,,	9	$1\frac{1}{2}$–2	7–9	7–$10\frac{1}{2}$	200–300
3	,, ,, ,, ,,	9	2	10	$10\frac{1}{2}$–13	300–360
4	,, Introduce solids	7	2	10	$12\frac{1}{2}$–15	350–420
5	Reduce bottle; increase solids	7			$14\frac{1}{2}$–18	400–500
6	Milk in bowl; solids	6			16–$21\frac{1}{2}$	450–600
7	Weaning completed	3			$19\frac{1}{2}$–25	550–700

A knowledge of the composition of cat's milk is useful when making up a cat's milk substitute for feeding orphaned or neglected kittens, or supplementing the deficient supply of a mother cat, especially when she is feeding more than four kittens. Cat's milk consists of 72 percent water, 9·5 percent protein, 6·8 percent fat, 10 percent carbo-hydrates and 0·75 percent minerals. Full-cream dried or unsweetened condensed cow's milk can be made up with warm water at double the strength recommended for human babies, which will give roughly the correct proportions for cats. Make sure that the milk powder is completely dissolved by using an electric whisk if necessary. An alternative mixture which dissolves more easily is double-strength skimmed milk powder (1oz in $\frac{1}{4}$ pint or 20g in 90ml water) to which 3 teaspoonfuls (15ml) of vegetable oil (e.g.

corn oil) is added and beaten at 100°F (37°C). Care must be taken to see that these mixtures do not become infected with bacteria; they should be made up at least every twenty-four hours and kept in a refrigerator when not in use. They should be fed at blood heat (37°C) by means of a glass pipette with a rubber teat, or preferably through one of the special glass cat feeding bottles available at good pet stores. Care must always be taken to prevent milk entering the windpipe; if this happens the kitten could die of pneumonia. The mixture should have additional vitamin A, 50µg (micrograms) per ml of milk substitute and a drop of vitamin E added. A proprietary mixture such as Abidec or Adexolin would be suitable. After feeding, an orphan kitten's rear must be gently stroked with a clean wisp of cottonwool to stimulate urination and defaecation. This substitutes for the washing action of the mother cat's tongue and unless carefully carried out the kitten will die due to urine retention. Goat's milk and egg yolk (never white) are also very beneficial to young kittens. The egg yolk should be beaten up with an equal quantity of water and used in place of other milk substitutes; it is especially useful for cats and kittens allergic to cow's milk. The size and number of feeds according to age and weight of the

kitten are given in the table. Solids can be introduced at about the fourth week and steps should be taken to encourage the kitten to lap milk from a small, unspillable receptacle. This can sometimes be done at three weeks by dipping your finger in the milk and rubbing it on the kitten's lips and tongue. Once kittens can lap, see that fresh water is always available.

Solids should consist of a variety of finely minced meat, cooked fish and other foods given to adult cats; soft canned cat foods are also suitable. Larger pieces should be given as the kitten learns to chew, so that when it is completely weaned at seven weeks it is able to take a nearly adult-type diet. Milk should be continued all the time, provided the kitten digests it well. Refusal to eat is the first sign that the cat is unwell and if refusal is continued for more than a day or two, a vet must be consulted. Kittens with infected, blocked noses are very unhappy since they cannot breathe through their mouths when they try to eat. They lose weight rapidly and their fur becomes bedraggled. A kitten which is being hand-reared should be regularly sponged and dried after feeding and remains of milk and other foods removed to leave the coat clean, dry and fluffy. This will help to maintain the health of the kitten.

Bottle-feeding an unweaned kitten. Use your thumb to control the flow of milk mixture from the special feeding bottle. Notice that the kitten is sitting up comfortably and sucking at the teat of its own free will; this ensures that the milk does not enter the lungs.

Training

All animals are creatures of habit. Habits, good and bad, are developed in youth and become progressively more difficult to break and reform as life proceeds so that a change of habit, which often goes with a change of environment, may be as disastrous for an elderly cat as for an elderly person. The most successful and happy individuals are undoubtedly those which, by their very training, remain relatively flexible and adaptable rather than rigid and limited. A well-trained but adaptable cat is a pleasure to have in the home whereas a cat that has been indulgently allowed to have its own way becomes a great trial to its owners and is viewed unfavourably by everyone else. Training principles which apply to young children apply equally to cats, which respond in a remarkable way to firmness coupled with kindness and consideration. Do not forget that the cat will expect to dominate in its territory but however much it overlords subordinates, you must make it quite clear that you will not allow it to dominate you.

TOILET TRAINING

Good mother cats carefully teach young kittens habits of cleanliness without any help from human beings. There are, however, good mothers and bad or neglectful mothers among cats, as there are among humans. The good mother, besides suckling her kittens at regular intervals, will thoroughly clean them with her tongue at each feed. Licking the anal region after a meal induces reflexes in the kitten resulting in urination and defaecation and this pattern can be followed in toilet training later on. Until the kitten can move around, the mother consumes all the waste products keeping the nest clean and dry. Since the reflexes for emptying the bladder and bowel have to be triggered early in life great care must be taken to set them in action in orphan kittens, or when the mother cat loses interest, by gently stroking the perineal region with a wisp of cottonwool after hand feeding. As soon as the kittens start scrambling around – at about three weeks – the mother cat starts toilet training; this is the time at which the human 'mother' should start toilet training. Soiling the nest is not permitted and kittens are shown where to urinate and defaecate following a meal, even to the extent of the mother picking them up by the scruff of the neck and placing them on a toilet tray or suitable patch of loose earth. Kittens rapidly form the habit of going to the same urination point which becomes recognizable to them by its scent mark. If, because no toilet tray is provided, kittens start to use the corner of a room at this stage, this likewise becomes scent marked and it becomes progressively more and more difficult to break the habit. Any re-training programme must involve very careful and thorough cleaning of the mis-used area finally treating it, if possible, with a strong-smelling disinfectant which will obscure the cat's own scent. When training an orphan kitten you should put it on the toilet tray from two and a half weeks onwards. If there is no result at first, make sure that you at least produce urination by stroking the perineal region with cottonwool as before but instead of throwing it away, bury it in the toilet tray to provide the correct scent and do not overclean or use strong smelling disinfectants to clean the toilet tray. The tray should be roughly 12 inches by 8 inches (30cm by 20cm) or larger, at least $2\frac{1}{2}$ inches (6cm) deep (preferably more) and should be made of plastic or tinned iron – a cheap roasting pan will do admirably. The latter will rust rapidly due to the acidity of the urine, however, so that a more expensive enamel pan may be a worthwhile investment. The tray should be filled with a clean, dry, absorbent material such as sawdust or peat, or a specially prepared cat litter can be purchased. Failing these, shredded newspaper is quite satisfactory. Whatever is used, it is a good idea to line the tray with newspaper so that the litter can be removed easily. Soiled litter can be put on the compost heap or burnt if you have a garden, or put in a

Do not ignore requests to go out unless the cat is courting! Cats quickly learn to operate latches within reach and cat flaps in doors.

plastic bag in the dustbin. It is extremely unwise to try to flush soiled litter down the lavatory as this will soon cause a blockage. Frequency of cleaning will depend on the depth of the tray and the number of cats using it. It should be changed when it becomes damp or when offensive odours are produced. In addition, flies should be discouraged. When scratching a hole in the litter the cat often scatters it outside the tray, and the tray must therefore be put on an easily cleaned surface such as a tiled floor,

or a floor with a lino or plastic covering, but never on a carpet. A tray with a wide, inward sloping lip helps to keep the litter inside and it is wise to place a sheet of newspaper beneath it. Never strike a kitten if it goes to the toilet in the wrong place. Simply speak harshly to it as you pick it up and place it on the tray. As you are doing this speak kindly to it. Animals respond very quickly to the tone of your voice, and the kitten will soon learn the correct places to perform its toilet.

It may be difficult to get a kitten or cat accustomed to using a toilet tray to transfer to the garden (or vice versa) and garden training should therefore be started in dry, preferably warm, weather. When the kitten has finished its meal, keep it away from the toilet tray and immediately take it near some freshly dug ground. When the kitten has performed in this way a couple of times it will only be necessary to put it outside the door after feeding. Remember that older kittens and cats urinate rather infrequently –

about once in twenty-four hours. They may defaecate even less regularly but this is not a cause for alarm. Increased frequency, straining or crying when attempting to urinate is a sign for *immediate* action; take the cat to the vet straight away. Owing to the tidy habits of cats it is difficult to inspect the faeces in the way you can for dogs. However, diarrhoea usually results in wet, bedraggled fur around the anus and steps should be taken to deal with the cause (see the chapter on ill health). Always watch for

Above Cats interested in 'forbidden' objects must be firmly reprimanded in a stern voice, reinforcing the reprimand with a light slap if necessary.
Right A roundworm. They can easily be distinguished from the flatter, segmented tapeworm. Piperazine drugs are effective in combating round-worms.

tapeworm and roundworm; the latter are more likely to be observed in vomit than in faeces. Worms, especially roundworms, are dangerous to children as well as debilitating to the cat. With the help of your vet, get rid of them! Moreover, insist that children do not allow kittens or cats to lick their faces and instruct them to wash their hands before meals it they have been playing with the cat. This will prevent any viable eggs from passing into the childrens' mouths.

DISCOURAGING TRESPASSING

Needless to say, cats should never be permitted to jump up on or lie on cots or prams at any time. A young cat can soon be taught not to jump on to tables or other furniture; one or two smart slaps will indicate that it has moved outside its permitted territory. This training will also discourage thieving as cats do not usually steal if they are well fed. It is unfair to leave a young cat alone with uncooked food on a table, however. Cats can also be easily trained in the same way to keep to their own baskets rather than occupy a human being's chair. Cat baskets or boxes should be kept clean, free from hairs and should be lined with an old, soft, washable blanket or towel or even newspaper.

TRAVELLING

Cats will adapt to travelling, especially if you start when they are young. They often prefer to sit freely in a car with which they are familiar but great care should be taken to ensure that they remain quiet and do not bother the driver. If in doubt always use a cat basket. Many people who visit weekend cottages or caravans regularly take their cat with them, and the cat adapts to its new home very quickly and does not seem to object at all to travelling to and fro by car. Travelling by public transport should *always* be done safely inside a cat basket or box since a cat is easily scared by noise, strange surroundings and strange people and may try to 'escape' – sometimes to be lost for ever, at other times to be accidentally killed. One of the most frightening places for a cat is a lift; the combination of noise and movement seems to be very disturbing. Some people successfully control their cats with a collar and lead but this must be well practised in normal, quiet surroundings

before going on a journey. Cats should not be taken for long walks like a dog. A cat may accompany you a certain distance of its own free will but it should never be forced to walk further than it wishes. For complete removal to a new home, it is best to keep the cat in an enclosed basket or box and to feed it only after arrival at the new house. The cat should be confined for a day or two until you are certain it will not try to return to the old territory.

HOLIDAYS

Finally, we come to the vexed question of holidays. The best solution is to keep the cat in its own home territory and arrange for a neighbour to come in and feed it daily. The main problem here is arranging access to the house for the cat, without encouraging the attentions of burglars. Remember also that an open door or window is an invitation to your cat's friends, particularly if you have a queen. If you have a garden, arrangements can be made, especially in summer, for the cat to use a shed which has a cat flap installed. Another solution is to find a close neighbour willing to take the cat altogether for the period of your absence. This can present more difficulty, since there is little doubt that a cat is more attached to its territory than to the people in it. Cats rarely pine for people but tend to be unhappy if displaced or taken to a boarding cattery. Only Feline Advisory Bureau recommended catteries should be chosen, or one recommended by someone who has had their cat there recently. The cattery must be very clean and ideally each cat should be kept in a separate enclosure from which it is unable to escape. In addition, veterinary advice must be readily available at the cattery. If you are using a particular cattery for the first time, ask to look round and only choose one which appears hygienic and well run. If you suspect that these criteria are not being met, look elsewhere; it is worth travelling further afield for the sake of both your cat's health and your peace of mind. Apart from the disruption caused by moving the cat to entirely strange surroundings, the main problem is the infectious diseases which can very easily be caught from other holiday boarders. To help prevent disease, you should ensure that your cat has been inoculated against all the common cat ailments.

Showing

Having read the chapter on choosing a cat, you may wish to consider the important question of showing. To do so, it is necessary to become familiar with the relevant rules and regulations which, although varying from country to country, all have a great deal in common. The procedure described below applies to exhibitors living in Britain but where American or continental practice differs significantly from the British, suitable explanatory information is given. One very important and basic difference is that in Britain the Governing Council of the Cat Fancy is the only body empowered to register and transfer cats and to grant show licences to its forty or so affiliated cat clubs, whereas in the United States and on the Continent there are many independent governing bodies each keeping their own register of cats and each staging their own shows. Furthermore American and continental shows always occupy two days, the first of which is devoted to judging the main classes and the second to making the best-in-show awards and distributing the prizes to the successful owners. This practice is made necessary by the great distances which cats and their owners often have to travel, and it is evident that under these conditions one-day shows would impose a very great strain on cat and exhibitor alike. In Britain, the distances involved are relatively short and the Council does not allow shows to last more than one day. The reason for this attitude is a humane one. Few cats enjoy the journey to and from the show and they enjoy the ordeal of being handled by judges and stewards and being stared at by the public even less. It is, of course, recognized that shows are marginally cruel. Equally it is recognized that they are necessary as an open forum for the comparison of cats, of breeding methods and of varietal popularity, as well as to provide a market place for kittens without which few but the very wealthy could afford to breed at all. In the opinion of the Governing Council the one-day show is the most humane compromise consistent with satisfying all of these needs.

The Council licenses three distinct types of show known in increasing order of importance as exemption shows, sanction shows and championship shows, and no British cat club may stage any of them without first obtaining Council approval of the chosen date and for the desired class of show.

Exemption shows are usually small, local affairs. In their running, many of the Council's most stringent show rules are relaxed and the management is not obliged to provide open classes for every recognized variety. Moreover, male and female cats may be shown in the same open classes and kittens of various ages and of either sex may compete against each other. The classes may be judged by probationer judges, and in some cases by very senior breeders. Indeed, the only rules which are very strictly enforced are those relating to vetting-in. Exemption shows are very often staged by comparatively new clubs and serve to provide their management with a great deal of useful experience which will later serve them well.

Sanction shows are run on exactly the same lines as championship shows except that championships are not awarded and a certain amount of class amalgamation is permitted. Their function is to serve as dress rehearsals on the strength of which a club may subsequently apply for a licence to run a championship show. The manner in which such shows are run and the conduct of the management are carefully observed, and in due course a report reaches the Council's executive committee which is the body empowered to grant show licences. Sanction and exemption shows are more or less an exclusively British institution. In the United States and on the Continent such shows are seldom, if ever, held.

Regulations for the running of championship shows are very strictly enforced and licences to hold such shows are only granted to clubs of great experience and long standing which have previously run several exemption and sanction shows in a satisfactory manner. Open classes, divided into

The National Cat Show, the most important date in the cat-showing calendar, but hard on the judges' feet! More than two thousand cats can normally be seen at this show.

Overleaf A team of senior judges choose the best-in-show from among the open class winners.

male and female categories, must be provided for every single recognized variety of cat, and kitten classes must be divided into age groups. Neuter classes for every major variety must also be made available. Championships are granted in Britain by the Governing Council, and on the Continent and in the United States by the governing bodies staging each show. Premierships are likewise awarded to neuter cats. The granting of championships (for entire cats) and premierships (for neutered cats) is entirely within the powers of open class judges who may withhold these awards if, in their opinion, the quality of the winner is not sufficiently high. Equally, a judge may award a championship even if there is only one exhibit in the class – provided it is of sufficiently high quality. In addition to open classes the show management may offer any number of side classes and, while open classes may only be judged by senior judges, side and kitten classes may also be judged by probationer judges. Club classes are also provided and their financial success is guaranteed by the clubs offering them as a service to their own members. Such classes may also be judged by junior or senior judges.

Formerly, prize money was always paid to the owners of cats placed first, second and third in open classes, but recently the Governing Council revoked the rule making this necessary. Very few clubs now pay prize money in such classes although money prizes are still paid in secondary classes which are either guaranteed, or else attract a large entry and are therefore always profitable. Prize money is never paid at continental and American shows.

To be eligible for exhibition, cats and kittens must be registered with the Council or with the appropriate ruling body on the Continent and in the United States. In the latter country cats registered with competitor clubs may still be shown provided they are also registered with the club staging the show. On the Continent, where the competition between the ruling bodies is regrettably less friendly, no cat may be registered with more than one ruling club and may not be shown at any show other than that sanctioned by the ruling body concerned. This makes for smaller entries, less friendly interchange of ideas and a somewhat restricted breeding programme, for

the veto applies also to the use of stud cats registered with another ruling body. It is to be hoped that this system will be reformed in time and will be reorganized on the more rational American pattern. As already stated, the problem does not occur in Britain because there is only one ruling body.

PROCEDURE AT SHOWS

On arrival at the show hall each exhibit is submitted to a strict veterinary inspection and, subject to being in good health and free from any trace of vermin, it may be penned by the exhibitor in a wire pen. This pen bears a number which corresponds to a tally worn around the exhibit's neck which was earlier sent to the exhibitor on receipt of his entrance form and fee. At British shows exhibitors are obliged to leave the hall before judging starts and the public is likewise not admitted into the hall until the afternoon, by which time judging of the open classes is completed. When the hall is cleared (in some halls exhibitors may watch the judging from balconies or from the sidelines on payment of a small fee) the judges, each accompanied by a steward pushing a trolley bearing towels and a wash basin or disinfectant spray, commence their work beginning with the open classes. Each cat in turn is removed from its pen by the steward and is presented to the judge for critical appraisal, the judge simultaneously writing comments in a judging book. When each cat in the class has been judged, the judge places the cats in order of quality after which a challenge certificate is awarded if, in the judge's opinion, the winning cat merits one.

In an open neuter class a premier certificate may likewise be awarded to the winner. Challenge and premier certificates are withheld in about fifteen percent of open classes. A cat which wins three challenge certificates under three different judges is granted championship status by the Council, and neuters likewise gain premier status. The judge enters his awards in the judging book in triplicate and two of the slips are taken up to the administrative table by the steward, the results being posted in the record book for the show. One slip is then mounted on a board by an official for examination by the exhibitors and the public. After the show the judges publish their results and comments in the Fancy's official journal. After

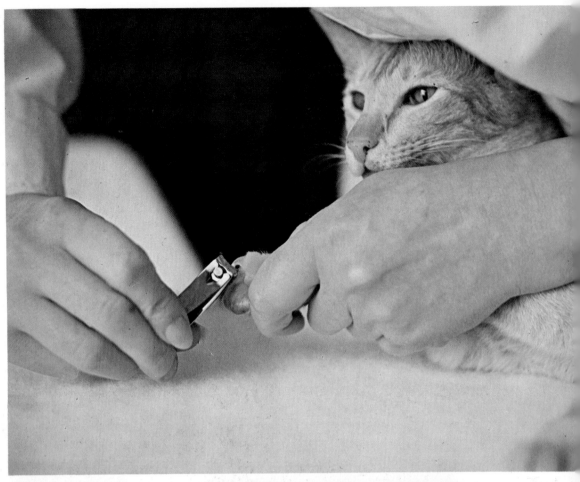

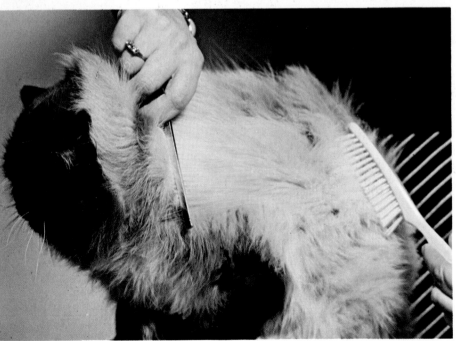

Above **This is the
correct way to cut a
cat's claws. Ensure that
only the tip is cut.
Left Using two combs
to groom a longhaired
cat prior to showing.
Right Rubbing the fur
of a shorthaired cat
with cottonwool helps
to leave the coat sleek
and glossy.**

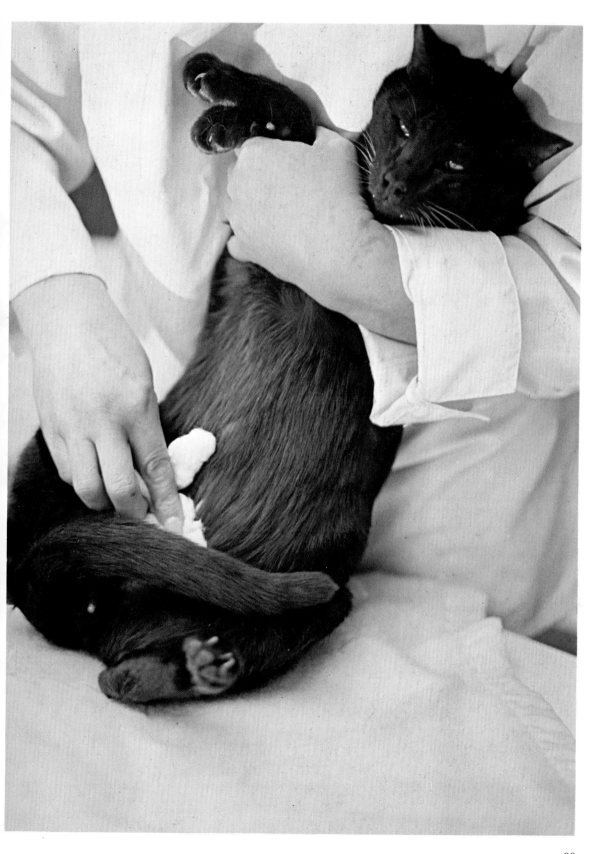

the exhibitors and the public are readmitted, the remainder of the day is spent by the exhibitors celebrating or bemoaning the results, feeding and caring for their cats, discussing cat politics, breeding methods and the latest news, and generally having a very enjoyable day. This is temporarily interrupted by the main spectacle of the occasion, the best-in-show judging. For this event the senior judges, either three or five in number, sit at a long table on the stage and select from among the principal winners of the day the best cats in their respective classes. Shows generally end at six o'clock in the evening and no exhibitor may remove a cat before the time of closure other than with the show manager's permission, which is only granted in exceptional cases.

On the Continent the procedure is different in that instead of going round to each pen the judges sit at a long table and have the cats brought to them by their stewards, while in America it is generally not the stewards but the owners who bring the cats to the judges for appraisal. The American procedure has often been criticized on the grounds that on seeing the owners, the judges may be improperly influenced when making their placings. Such a criticism is difficult to support. Judges are exalted persons in the Cat Fancies of the world. Having reached their position, they have nothing to fear and nothing to lose by being perfectly objective. Moreover, although the owner's name is not disclosed at European shows it is fair to say that most judges, with their highly trained eye, easily recognize many of the prominent exhibits. The integrity of judges must be beyond question if the Fancies of the world are to retain their excellent image in the public mind. American judges are professional and are paid a fee for their services. European judges are not paid a fee but receive their out-of-pocket expenses. It is customary, however, for the clubs which invite judges to officiate at their shows to provide accommodation for them and to make their stay as enjoyable as possible.

SHOW PREPARATION

There is a rare phenomenon in the cat world known as a flyer. This is a cat which is so outstanding that it will win even if recovered from a duck pond five minutes before a show. Such cats are rare indeed, and most of them have a very much better chance of winning if expertly groomed and prepared. The principle underlying the practice of grooming is the same for all varieties of cat – scrupulous cleanliness followed by expert coat preparation – but the method of achieving the latter depends upon the nature of the coat. Cleanliness of the coat is best achieved by dry cleaning or by washing. On the whole, the former method is the one to be preferred unless the coat is very dirty indeed. Dry cleaning is best carried out by first combing the coat to take out any knots or adhesions and then rubbing into it a quantity of warm bran or ponderous magnesium carbonate which has previously been warmed in an oven at about 300°F (150°C) and allowed to cool until the back of the hand may comfortably be held against it. The warming process must be continued for not less than twenty minutes to expel all adsorbed moisture. Half an hour later the coat must be brushed and combed to remove the cleaner used. If the coat is very dirty it may be necessary to repeat the process. Washing, if felt to be necessary, is best carried out with warm, softened or rain water and soft or baby soap. After washing, the coat must be thoroughly rinsed in soft water and dried, either with a warm towel or, if the cat does not object, with a hair dryer. Never use a hair dryer if the cat is at all frightened by it.

The next process will depend upon the nature of the coat and it will be assumed that the cleaning has been carried out by either the wet or the dry methods described above.

Longhaired cats must appear massive in the show pen with the hair behind the ears curling upwards, the tail well furnished and the tufts on the feet prominent. This effect may be produced by combing with a plastic comb and brushing with a nylon-bristled brush. On no account should a metal comb or brush be used to groom a longhaired cat. The principle underlying this method relies upon the fact that dry fur is a very poor conductor of electricity. This may easily be verified by stroking a cat which is warming itself near a fire. If the hand is dry and clean a spark will be heard. It may be difficult to believe that the potential difference causing the spark may be several hundred volts, but this can easily be proved. When brushing and combing clean, dry fur with a nylon comb and brush, a static charge of electricity is induced in it, and a coat so charged with electricity will cause each individual hair to stand apart from the others thus giving the much desired appearance of massive splendour. The combing and brushing process should finally be carried out when placing the cat in its pen just prior to judging. In doing this, gloves should be worn. Great care must be exercised to be sure of removing every trace of powder from the coat as failure to do so could lead to the disqualification of the cat.

Siamese and other foreign shorthairs require a different treatment to make the coat sleek, glossy and close-lying. After dry cleaning or washing and drying as described above, the coat must be subjected to prolonged hand grooming and combing with a steel comb. The human hand always has a fine layer of oil on its surface, together with a trace of salt. The first of these ingredients imparts a glossiness to the coat and the second makes it a good conductor of electricity which, together with the steel comb, discharges all the static electricity present thus making it possible for the hairs to lie side by side without any mutual repulsion. This condition of coat is just right for producing the desired glossy and close-lying appearance sought by judges. A little baby powder or talc dusted into the coat just prior to penning, followed by a good combing and brushing with steel equipment, will ensure that the cat is at its best when judged a few minutes later, in its open class. One word of warning: cats with black or very dark fur should not be treated with powder just before a show. It is difficult to remove the last traces of powder and the judge will take a very dim view of any remaining in the coat. British-type cats require little more than dry cleaning, or bathing and drying if very dirty, followed by a good brushing on the morning of the show. Their coats have just the right length and texture to show well with the minimum of preparation.

Apart from the coat, the eyes and ears of a cat may need some attention. Eyes may be gently wiped with a soft, linen handkerchief moistened with a proprietary brand of eye-cleansing lotion or with boracic lotion, and the ears are best cleaned with cottonwool buds moistened with olive oil. On no account should the inexperienced exhibitor or breeder attempt to clean deep inside the ear. The presence of deeply seated dirt could indicate canker in which case a veterinary surgeon should be consulted. Claws which are excessively long may be trimmed with nail clippers but care should be taken not to use them too enthusiastically or to crush or fracture them. It is best to seek the advice of a vet before attempting this for the first time. No amount of expert grooming will transform a bad show cat into a good one, but all things being equal, the well-groomed cat will win every time.

SHOWING STUD CATS
An entire male cat is a proud and delightful animal which is constrained by his tendency to spray, to a life of segregation in a cat house. However comfortable his quarters may be his owner should always remember that he is not a wild animal and that he needs human companionship and affection like any other pet. The owner should visit him several times daily (and not only at mealtimes) and should spend as much time as possible with him to let him know that he is loved. A stud cat brought up in this way will become gentle and unafraid of being handled; and consequently will offer no objection to being taken out of his pen by stewards or to being handled by judges. A cat which cannot be handled cannot be judged and many fine cats lose all chances of a championship because their owners show them insufficient affection and they become unaccustomed to people and afraid of being handled by strangers at the shows.

TAKING CATS TO AND FROM SHOWS
Many people travel considerable distances to and from the shows and it is most important to ensure that cats make the journey in comfort and under draught-free conditions. There are no problems with cats which are accustomed to travel 'loose' inside their owners' cars but if a cat is to be transported by train or by any other method of public transport it is essential that it should travel in a suitable basket. The best kind of cat container consists of a wooden base surmounted by a perspex dome equipped with adequate ventilation holes at the top and near the base. Such containers are virtually draught-proof and may be bought at all the principal shows. They have the further

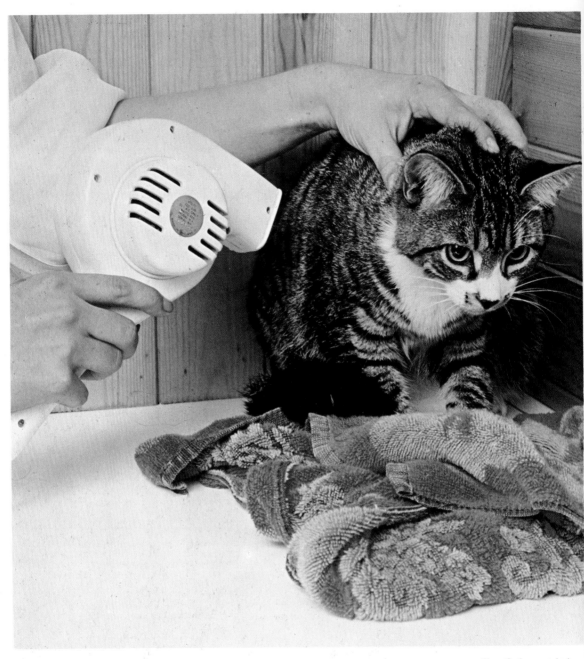

Above **Only use a hair dryer if the cat does not object.**
Top right **Judging an Abyssinian.**
Right **A National Cat Show winner with rosettes.**

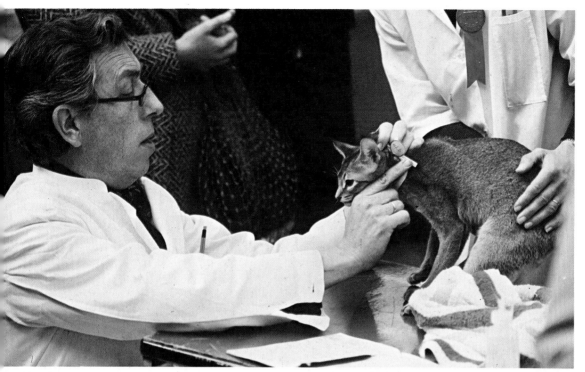

advantage that the cat's view of the outside world is not obstructed and it is therefore far less likely to become frightened or claustrophobic. If an ordinary wicker cat basket is used the floor should be lined with a warm blanket or with a whole folded newspaper while the sides should be externally wrapped with brown paper held securely in place with adhesive tape or string. The top should be left uncovered to provide adequate ventilation.

Sending cats to a show by aeroplane or rail is most unusual in Britain where the show rules require the cat to be accompanied by the owner or by the owner's representative. On the Continent and in the United States where great distances are often involved cats are frequently dispatched alone, their owners having arranged that someone should meet the train or aeroplane and take the cat to the show. When a cat is dispatched alone in this manner it is essential that its basket be provided with two securely tied labels each bearing the name, address and telephone number of the sender and of the recipient. Two labels are necessary in case one of them accidentally becomes detached.

Should any delay or mishap occur in transit this practice will ensure that the cat's arrival at its destination is delayed as little as possible. In addition, the sender should always inform the recipient by telephone or telegram the time of the cat's actual departure and estimated arrival at its destination. It is always a good practice for the sender to ask the porter or stewardess in charge of the cat to keep a special eye on it. Most people are naturally kind to animals and will prove helpful if made aware of the cat's presence.

JUDGES AND STEWARDS

It is not easy to become a cat judge. It is necessary to have bred cats for at least seven years, to have benched many winners and to have stewarded for a great number of senior judges. In addition, a judge must be a person of high integrity and must have the right kind of temperament. British judges are nominated either by the committees of specialist clubs or by joint committees selected by groups of clubs. Selection is not conducted by examination but rather by discussion among the selectors, most of whom are senior judges themselves. This method may give the appearance of being somewhat

unreliable but it should be remembered that the British Cat Fancy is a very close-knit community in spite of its 8000-strong membership and the kind of person who is likely to seek election to the office of judge will be intimately known to those who will consider his or her application. In recent years the Siamese clubs have formed a joint committee which, in its turn, has elected a judge-appointing panel made up of senior judges. Candidates who satisfy the minimum requirements of breeding, showing and stewarding may have their application considered by this committee. Similarly, the longhair clubs have recently formed their own joint committee and judges panel. No doubt the other specialist clubs will soon form their own equivalent bodies. Nominations made by these panels or by specialist clubs have to go before the Council for approval and, if approval is granted, the newly made judge becomes an officer of the Council and is greatly respected in the Fancy.

Judges of Siamese cats are qualified to judge all the varieties of Siamese, but judges of longhairs may only judge those varieties for which they have been specifically approved. This practice has often been severely criticized by the judges themselves, for while each variety of longhaired cat is to some degree different from other varieties, the differences are generally small, and it should be no problem for a judge to acquire the minor additional skills needed to judge every variety of longhaired cat. At present, a judge may be allowed to judge blue persians but not black or white persians and it is felt by many experienced judges and breeders that such a limitation on the potential services of a judge is wholly unjustified. The opposing argument put forward is that the system makes for a very high degree of specialization because of which British judges are considered very highly throughout the world. It is perhaps significant that every continental club invites British judges to officiate at its shows, gladly paying the considerable expenses involved.

In the United States and on the Continent judges are appointed on the basis of a series of examinations and, if successful, become either longhair or shorthair judges. The former are then qualified to judge all varieties of longhair, and the latter all varieties of shorthair including the Siamese. Each of these systems has something to recommend it, and no doubt their relative merits will be debated for many years.

WHAT DO JUDGES LOOK FOR AT SHOWS?

The forty or so recognized varieties of cat each has an approved standard of points as already explained on pages 42–63. In theory, the judge examines each cat and awards points for each of its features depending upon the importance of each particular feature as defined in the standard laid down for that variety. Again in theory, the winning cat is the one gaining the highest aggregate of points. In practice few, if any, judges employ the points system as the basis of assessment for the simple reason that to do so would be virtually impossible. It is true that a certain number of points can be given for each of a number of isolated qualities capable of being measured in relation to a subjective scale. If this is done a winning cat may be found to possess a head, body, coat and legs all of which are perfect whereas the proportion between them is very wrong. A good judge is born and not created and although the experience gained by breeding, showing and stewarding is undeniably of the greatest value it can never be as valuable as the possession of a natural 'eye' for a cat. It would be true to say that most experienced judges use the standards of points only as a background of prescribed reference for assessing the relative values or faults in the different varieties of cat. How many points to award for such indefinable qualities as superb proportion, outstandingly graceful carriage, the ripple of silken muscle or the proud glance in the eye of a superb, healthy animal endowed with grace and vitality can be decided by the trained judge but may never adequately be expressed by words or numbers. Years of practice may make a competent judge, but the great judges have the gift of appreciating beauty.

The author, an international judge and formerly chairman of the Governing Council of the Cat Fancy, examining a superb blue-eyed white longhair.

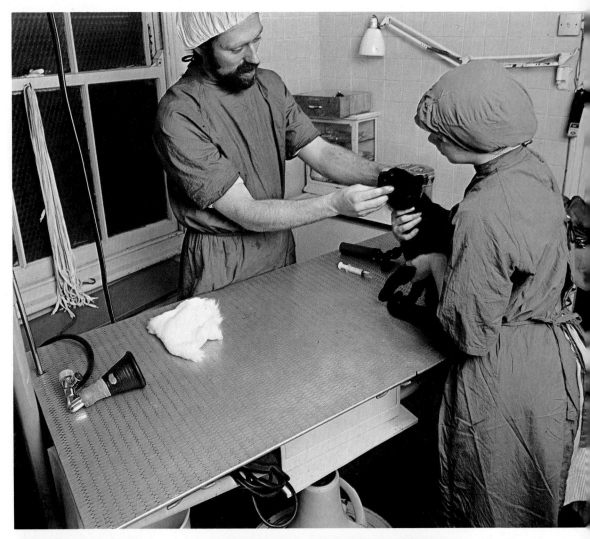

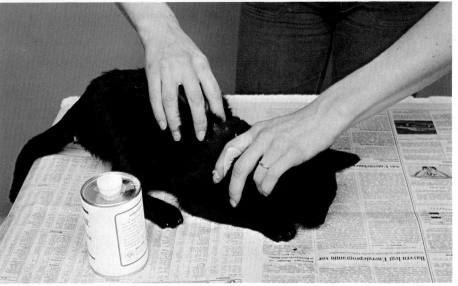

Above A veterinary surgeon and his nursing assistant examining a cat prior to administering a general anaesthetic.

Left Rubbing a safe insecticidal powder into a cat's coat, making sure that it is rubbed down to the skin against the lie of the hair. Do remember to brush out any excess powder after half an hour thus preventing the cat from swallowing an excess when grooming itself.

Right A vet giving a subcutaneous injection into the scruff of a cat's neck.

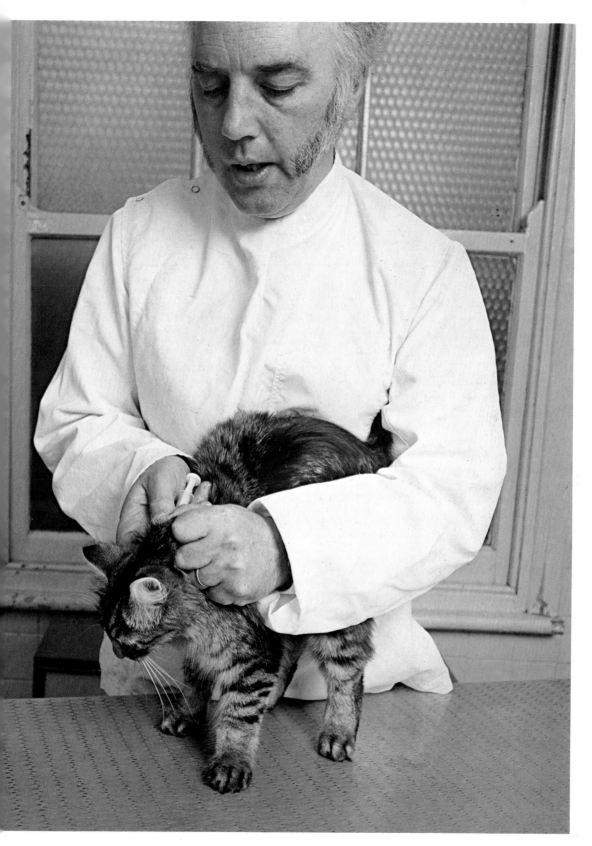

Ill health and home nursing

If your cat had its eyelids glued together with dry pus, its nose caked solid with mucus and thick, mucoid saliva drooling from its mouth you would realize that it was ill and take it to your veterinary surgeon. You should, however, have been able to recognize that your cat was ill several days earlier. This chapter, then, has two main aims: firstly to provide an aid to the recognition of ill health in the cat and secondly to advise on the best methods of nursing a cat, particularly a very ill cat. Early recognition of disease, and consequent treatment of the disease by a veterinary surgeon in its early stages, can so often lead to a quick recovery. For instance, if the owners had taken the flu case described above to their veterinary surgeon when the cat first sneezed the disease would probably have lasted only a few days. Now, however good the veterinary surgeon, the disease will last at least three weeks and the cat could die unless properly nursed.

Despite domestication the cat can be a most reserved animal. Many are reluctant to show their owners that they are ill, preferring to go away secretly and hide. It is no good thinking that your cat is ill every time that it is away from home, however. It may be visiting friends, soaking up the sun or merely sleeping off the effects of a morning's successful hunting – a full stomach of fur, feather or fish. Undue worry will cause *you* to become ill instead.

With few exceptions, the first sign of ill health in a cat is loss of appetite. The opposite is even more true; that is, if the cat is eating normally there is little wrong with it. Most of the occasions when a cat is off food but still healthy can be attributed to a desire to mate. A full tom may stay away for days on end and return thin and bedraggled after serenading a confined and therefore unobtainable loved one. He may also return with a split ear and a mauled body having battled with other suitors. These superficial wounds can be bathed with a dilute anti-

septic but in general the cat's own tongue is a far more efficient cleaner of such wounds and the cat is better left alone. If, however, one of the other suitors managed to inflict a severe bite, the needle-sharp canine teeth may have carried some of the hair well below the skin. In this case your tom, instead of giving himself a manly shake and demanding large quantities of food, will appear lethargic and go off his food on either

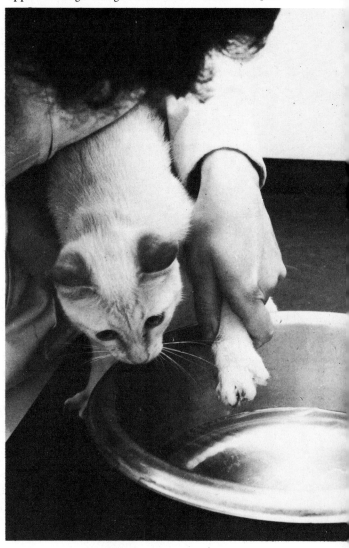

A swollen toe due to infection following a bite received during a fight with another cat. Fomenting the toe by bathing it in warm water is a useful first aid and helps to draw the pus.

the second or third day after his return, signifying that an abscess is developing. Off to the vet with him! In fact many owners, having visited their veterinary surgeons a number of times with such shameless toms, decide that it is a matter of 'off to the vet' for another purpose. The only cure is castration or old age. The queen also loses her interest in food when in season. There is a tremendous variation in behaviour at this time: many roll on the ground in a most sinuous, sexy manner; others 'pedal' continuously with their hind quarters close to the ground; a few are silent; most are noisy giving almost continuous cries of invitation, and a few, particularly Siamese, create such a noise that the owner may need to resort to ear plugs. These are all signs of a perfectly healthy queen, and if her desires are not

satisfied she may well 'come back' and start it all over again in a few weeks' time. No wonder that many owners prefer the neutered animal.

So your cat is off its food and it is not craving for the opposite sex. Does it seem otherwise normal and happy? If so, wait and watch for twenty-four hours. It may well be suffering from some mild digestive upset. This is particularly common in longhaired cats which, following the well-known rule 'when in doubt, wash!' ingest a considerable quantity of hair. Occasionally some of this hair gets caught in the throat causing the cat to cough, whilst at other times it reaches the stomach and may form a fur ball too large for comfortable passage from there into the bowel. Some cats can vomit at will and these often bring up a

queen calling. Some queens take up this posture when they are in season.

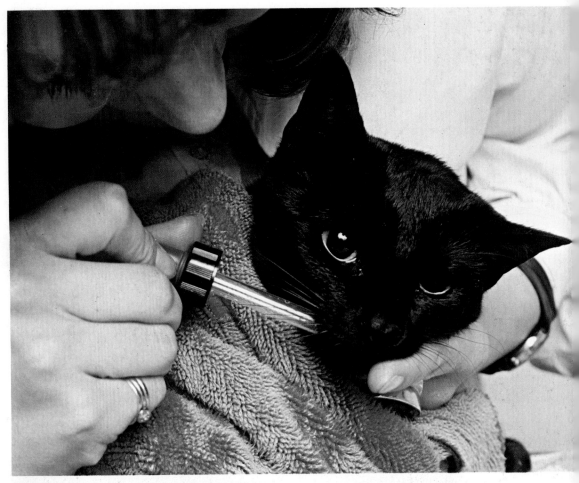

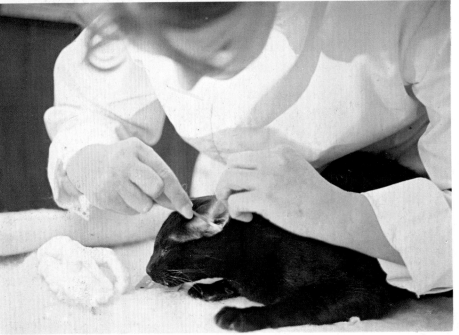

Above A cat being giv
liquid medicine, a
couple of drops at a
time, from a dropper
Note that the cat has
been wrapped in a so
towel so that any
attempts to use its
claws are frustrated.
Left Cleaning a cat's
ears using a soft
cottonwool bud on th
end of a pliable stick.
Right A registered
animal nursing
auxiliary (RANA)
applying two or three
drops of commercial
available ear drops to
cat's ears.

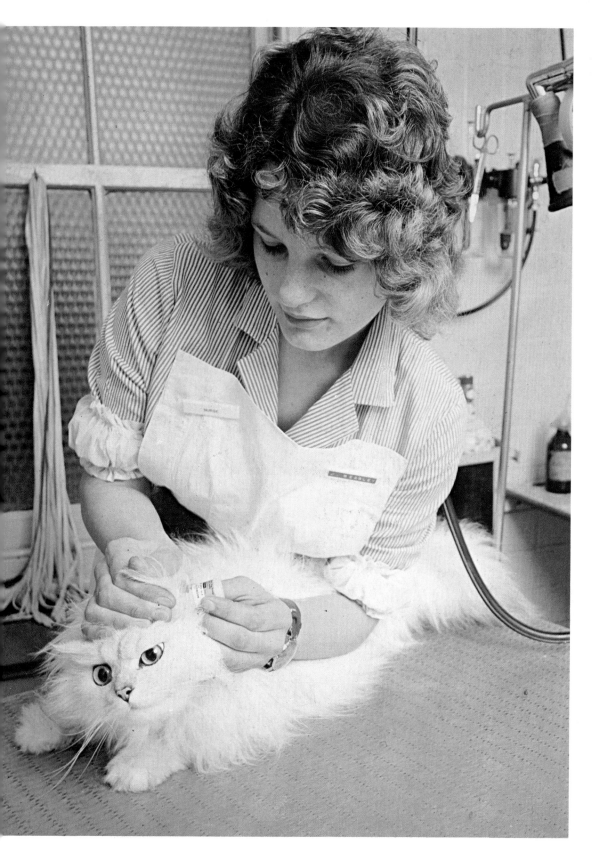

small amount of hair mixed with mucus and deposit it on the floor. Others, given the opportunity, will eat grass, its coarse nature irritating the stomach and causing vomiting. In some cases a fur ball manages to pass into the intestine where it may produce a feeling of discomfort or even severe constipation. In the majority of cases, particularly in young cats, the condition rights itself but if you have an old cat prone to this condition, it is a good idea to mix a little liquid paraffin or olive oil (about one teaspoonful) in with the food. Never use castor oil and never pour liquid paraffin down a cat's throat for it is so bland that occasionally it beats even the cat's excellent gag reflex and goes down the wrong way into the windpipe. Of course, the best way to prevent a fur ball is to groom the cat regularly and here the co-operation of the cat must be considered.

It is frequently said that books on cats give very little advice on first aid and that the words 'take the cat to the veterinary surgeon' often appear. I am afraid that this book is no exception. This is not simply because vets are specialists trained in dealing with sick animals but also because the feline is not a co-operative patient and veterinary surgeons have two indispensable aids to their treatment which are not available to the general public, namely anaesthetics and antibiotics. Your cat may allow you to tug the knots out of its coat – this simply means that it is accustomed to regular grooming and accepts it as part of its natural life – but other cats will bite and scratch. Your cat may allow you to clean its ears and cut its nails – this simply means that you are an owner with a good relationship with your cat – but others will resent even these painless attentions. For a cat to accept treatment involving pain, even the cleansing of wounds or the removal of a foreign body from a paw is unusual, however. Indeed, it is usually only a very ill cat that will tolerate it. Therefore you must use restraint or anaesthesia. My advice is do not try and use restraint. A struggling cat, and in particular a young cat of three to eight months, can break its own back by its efforts to get free and a sick animal will exhaust its last reserves and die in your arms as you struggle to get a teaspoonful of medicine into it. The veterinary surgeon has at his disposal a large range of simple and safe anaesthetics under which the cat has

no option other than to co-operate and also a range of antibiotics which are effective against the majority of cat germs. The suggestion 'take it to the vet' is not a slur on your intelligence but rather an acknowledgement of the fact that cats, unlike dogs, rarely trust their owners to know best. It is still useful, however, to be able to recognize the signs of some of the common disease conditions affecting the cat, and a number are described below.

LICKING OR GULPING MOTIONS

These may be due to either tonsillitis which frequently precedes an attack of flu, or to a sore mouth. Sore lips in kittens and young cats are frequently the result of unwary investigation of irritant liquids such as bleach or strong disinfectants. These usually heal themselves, but it is wise to have a look inside the mouth to see whether it is similarly burnt. It is very rare, however, for even a kitten to swallow any such irritant and even if the mouth is burnt recovery is usually rapid. Encourage the patient to take liquids or pap foods as the mouth will obviously be too sore for solids for a few days.

If the licking and gulping motions are accompanied by excessive salivation the cat is probably suffering from ulcerative glossitis (basically a sore tongue), which is due to a virus similar to those that cause cat flu. If you look into the mouth you will see raw areas on the tongue forming a crescent moon or horseshoe shape. The cat should be taken to the vet at once, but may also require a great deal of home nursing as described later.

A sore mouth may also be caused by bad teeth. In many cases this is really the fault of the diet, for a semi-wild farm cat living on natural prey is far less likely to have bad teeth than a domestic pet. The discomfort is usually due to a build up of tartar. Tartar is composed of calcium phosphate and is very porous. Bacteria, from both the mouth and the food, multiply in the tartar and can make the mouth very smelly. The tartar causes the gums to become inflamed so that a red line can be seen along the gum line and it may also force the gums to recede as the build up of tartar on the tooth extends towards the root. Such teeth become loose and may fall out. Once the tartar has formed

cat with an eosino-
hilic granuloma of the
p. Prompt treatment
ill prevent the condi-
on progressing this
r.

there is little that you can do except take the cat to the vet who will then chip the tartar off under a general anaesthetic. It is another case of prevention being better than cure and if your cat has no access to natural prey and eats nothing except what you yourself provide, *do* occasionally provide a large, raw bone and *do not* feed only tinned pap.

Sometimes the gulping motion is due to trouble further back in the throat. Cats are inquisitive creatures and threaded needles left in armchair rests or an open needle case can be an invitation to trouble. Once the cotton thread is in the mouth, the backward

pointing villi on the tongue force it further back and into the throat. Unfortunately, the needle sometimes gets drawn in too and usually becomes lodged in the throat. You may be able to locate the needle by looking in your cat's mouth but unless you have that rare, co-operative cat it is once again a job for the vet. One golden rule: if you can see just a cotton thread, *do not* pull it. It may be the only way in which your vet can locate the buried needle.

The cat has one mouth lesion which is unique to the species, an eosinophilic granuloma of the upper lip, often mistakenly called a rodent ulcer. Cats' tongues are very rough due to the many backward-pointing villi, and once a lesion has begun the cat is constantly licking the sore and irritating the tissue that is trying to form a scar. At first it looks like a small, shiny area, usually on the upper lip but sometimes involving the tongue. Attention from the vet is necessary or it will spread rapidly like the one shown and treatment becomes difficult.

VOMITING

In the healthy cat, occasional vomiting is nothing more than a wilful act to relieve an uncomfortable stomach by the simplest method possible. As already mentioned, some cats vomit fur balls; others eat their food too quickly, feel uncomfortable, and bring it all up in order to settle down and re-eat it more slowly.

Vomiting in a sick cat is serious. It can indicate severe disease of almost any organ in the body, and the condition should be investigated by the vet. In such cases, however, it is not usually a primary symptom. Once, vomiting was often a symptom associated with feline infectious enteritis (F.I.E.), otherwise known as panleuco-paenia. The disease is caused by a virus which is difficult to kill and has been known to remain viable on infected premises for at least a year. Although vomiting frequently occurs in a mild attack of F.I.E., the disease is commonly so severe that the cat is found dead without the owner having noticed any signs of disease. Anyone who owns a cat should ensure it is inoculated against this disease. The age at which vaccination should be given varies slightly with the circumstances. If the queen has been recently vaccinated she will give a passive immunity to her kittens whilst they are suckling and this immunity will last for a few weeks after weaning. To be absolutely safe, vaccinate at eight weeks and again at about three and a half months. Thereafter, booster vaccines should be given every two years.

DIARRHOEA AND CONSTIPATION

If your cat makes a mess all over the floor, the cause is most likely to be something it has eaten and this is best treated by with-holding all solid food for the next twenty-four hours. If the diarrhoea persists, a simple kaolin and liquid paraffin mixture

A male cat that is constantly adopting this 'yoga' position and licking round his penis and prepuce may have urethritis (inflammation of the lining of his urethra) or he may be having severe difficulty in passing urine because of a partial or complete urethral obstruction.

can be obtained from most chemists and this usually eases the condition. Certain cats cannot tolerate some foods. Many cannot digest fresh milk as they lack a specific enzyme in their digestive system and drinking milk results in profuse, though transient, diarrhoea. This is seen most commonly in kittens from about ten weeks old and particularly in Siamese cats. Some foods, such as fresh offal (particularly liver), are also inclined to cause diarrhoea but in this case the difficulty may be overcome by introducing the food slowly. Feed only an ounce (about 30 grams) or so of the fresh offal mixed in with the cat's usual diet to start with and then gradually increase the amount of offal. Persistent diarrhoea is rare in the cat. In tropical countries it is associated with hookworm infestation but this is very rare in Britain. Chronic diarrhoea may occur in debilitated cats which have been ill for some time, when it can be due to a lack of vitamin A. It also occurs, but rarely, in association with a form of cancer.

Constipation has already been mentioned in connection with fur balls. Another cause is malformation of the pelvis associated with a condition called juvenile feline osteo-dystrophy. One teaspoonful (5 ml) of liquid

When passing urine normally, a cat has the point of his hocks and his prepuce very near the soil or litter, his back fairly straight and a satisfied expression on his face.

Urine is not flowing and the cat is exerting more abdominal pressure. He has raised his hocks and curved his back. Many owners associate this position with that of a cat that is passing faeces. Do not dash for the castor oil, but look at your cat carefully and see if there are any white crystals on his prepucial hairs. Does he get into the yoga position or does he keep returning to attempt to pass urine? Any or all of these signs means that your cat is in severe trouble and you must take him to your veterinary surgeon.

paraffin mixed with the food daily is the recommended treatment.

STRAINING

When you see your cat straining on its dirt box, do not dash for the liquid paraffin. Watch. It is likely, particularly if the cat is a male, that he is not constipated but having difficulty in passing urine. This difficulty is associated with a condition called urolithiasis, which literally means stones in the urinary tract. In the cat these stones are in three forms: compressed plugs of crystals in the urethra; small stones about $\frac{1}{12}$ of an inch (2 millimetres) in diameter called microcalculi; or larger stones called calculi in the bladder.

In the male cat, whether entire or neutered, the problem is usually in the urethra and there are a number of signs for which you should watch. The cat may suddenly start to be dirty around the house, urinating elsewhere than in his tray, or he may urinate much more frequently than usual. He may also persistently wash himself in the area of his prepuce and penis. These are all signs of discomfort. Once an actual blockage has occurred the cat makes constant attempts to pass urine, often assuming an unnatural position in order to exert maximum abdominal pressure. At this time he looks anxious and often peers round towards his flank. He may give short cries of pain and may continue to wash himself excessively in a 'yoga' position. Sometimes white plugs of crystals can actually be seen on the preputial hairs.

Once blockage has occurred this is obviously a matter for the veterinary surgeon, but there are a number of things which the owner can do to relieve the condition in its early stages and also to prevent recurrence. In nine out of ten cases the blockage is caused by crystals of struvite (magnesium ammonium phosphate) and cats suffering from this should be fed a diet low in magnesium. A list of such foodstuffs, some of which are acceptable to cats suffering from urolithiasis, is given below. A list of foodstuffs rich in magnesium, which should therefore be avoided whenever possible, is also given. There are various other ways in which the formation of these struvite crystals can be inhibited and your veterinary surgeon may give you some tablets to change the acidity of the urine if he thinks that this is desirable. It is also advisable to make the urine more dilute simply by adding water to the food. Every meal should be mashed up with about 2 tablespoonfuls (30ml) of water. In addition, fresh water should be available at all times.

Foodstuffs of low magnesium content

Foodstuff	Magnesium in mg per 100 g food	Comments
Beef dripping	trace	High calorific value
Boiled cabbage	6·3	Useful bulk
Boiled carrots	6·4	Useful bulk
Boiled marrow	6·7	Useful bulk and increased water
Boiled rice	4·4	Useful bulk
Butter	2·4	Source of vitamin A
Cream cheese	5·2	
Fried cod roe	10·5	
Fried herring roe	8·1	
Milk	14·0	All milk products are safe
Raw bacon	10–12	Varies with fat content
Luncheon meat	9·4	Use a 'spam' based luncheon meat. Pork luncheon meat is high in magnesium
Stewed tripe	7·9	
Scrambled egg	12·0	The yolk is more beneficial than the white

Foodstuffs of high magnesium content

Foodstuff	Magnesium in mg per 100 g food	Comments
Beef	25·0	Minced raw beef has been proved to be harmful as the magnesium content is high and the calcium content very low
Heart	19·7	
Pork	26·0	
Cod	26·0	Similar figures recorded for other filleted white fish
Herring	34·7	
Kippers	47·0	
Pilchards	38·0	
Sardines	41·0	
Chicken (boiled)	26·4	This value falls in roast chicken

Some dried cat foods have a high magnesium content and should never be fed to stone-forming cats.

PAIN ON HANDLING

The cat's reaction to pain is sometimes minimal, as in the adult cat with a fractured leg which, if left undisturbed, may well appear quite comfortable. At other times, particularly in the kitten, the reaction is almost hysterical and a well-recognized instance of this hysteria is in the kitten suffering from juvenile feline osteodystrophy. Here, as a result of improper feeding, the kitten's bones are paper thin and fractures occur spontaneously. The kitten may merely leap or jump off a low footstool and in so doing break its leg, or arch its back and break one of the vertebrae. The most common type of improper feeding that produces this condition is minced beef and milk and nothing else. Either due to the price of beef or to education of the cat-loving public, this condition is now less common. If you should find a kitten struggling on the floor screaming and biting at everything within reach, pick it up by the scruff of its neck, put it in a small cardboard box and place it in a dark, warm place. It is no use taking it to the vet at this stage and it is amazing how many of these back injuries can and do make a spontaneous recovery after rest. Unfortunately, as was mentioned earlier, many of the recovered cases are left with a deformed pelvis and may suffer from constipation.

There is another distinctive pain cry which is associated with peritonitis, and which used to be heard most commonly in cases of F.I.E. This is a plaintive cry which the cat gives when any pressure is exerted on the abdomen, and which is usually noticed when the cat is lifted bodily with a hand under the tummy. This is, of course, a serious condition requiring veterinary attention.

SKIN CONDITIONS

There are a number of disease conditions when the cat cannot be truly described as ill, and which in many cases can be treated by the owner. Almost all of them are related to the skin. The cat suffers from a large number of parasitic infections such as fleas, lice, notoedric mites, cheyletiella, harvest mites (trombicula) and otodectic mites.

One of the odd things, however, is the extraordinary difference in the reaction to these parasites shown by different cats. For instance, a farmyard cat may be crawling with fleas and yet show little discomfort whereas a domestic Persian may throw an eczematous reaction to the presence of one flea. Nor is this simply a matter of breed or pedigree, for the Persian's own brother or sister in the same household may be as indifferent to a high flea burden as the farmyard cat.

Fleas, as many people know, are small, brown creatures which run close to the skin under the coat and jump violently to take avoiding action when off the animal. The lush, long, silky coat of a Persian-type cat provides a perfect habitat for a flea and if there is only a small population in residence it may be difficult to locate the insect. Flea dirt is easily recognizable, however, as small, brownish black particles similar to soot, lying close to the skin. The flea is a blood-sucking animal and this excreta is full of haemoglobin, so if you wish to determine conclusively whether the particles are soot or flea dirt place a few of them on a damp piece of paper and a reddish ring of haemoglobin will appear around each speck if it is flea dirt.

Fleas are by far the most common reason for an 'itchy' cat – the cat whose skin quivers when you only touch it gently. These cats often lick themselves so much that large areas of the coat become thinned, particularly the areas over the back and down the loins. Between washes they sit and twitch, and often growl for no apparent reason. Such cats may show an eczematous reaction. The word eczema simply means an inflammation of the skin, which usually takes the form of a small, red rash. For many years it was thought that there was a specific type of eczema in the cat associated with the feeding of too much fish, but it is now realized that almost every case of eczema in the cat is due to an allergic reaction to fleas. Untreated cats develop encrusted pustules all over the body, which necessitates treatment with antibiotics as well as measures aimed at removal of the parasites. It has recently been found that certain modern synthetic hormones can relieve this hypersensitivity fairly rapidly.

Most animals have their own specific flea and the cat is no exception. Cat fleas like to

'eat cat' and human fleas like to 'eat human', but this does not mean that occasionally a less fastidious flea will not take a bite of the wrong species. Such fleas seldom stay on an unnatural host for long, however, and even if your cat comes home one evening with its face covered with hedgehog fleas they will all have left it by the next day. Fleas do not breed on animals; they breed in cracks and crevices, preferably in wood, and it is this that makes their elimination so difficult. You must treat both the animal and its habitat.

There are two golden rules for the treatment of a cat with a flea infestation, or indeed with any external parasite. First, make sure that any insecticidal dressing that you use is made specifically for use on the cat. Many modern insecticides are far more dangerous to a cat than, for example, to a dog, partly because a cat will ingest a considerable part of any dressing left in the coat whilst washing. The second rule is not to use any form of insecticide in oil or in conjunction with an oily ointment, as this increases the absorption and therefore the toxicity of the insecticide.

There are four common methods of dealing with a flea infestation.
1. Bathing the cat in an insecticidal bath specially made for cats. This is probably the most effective treatment and the safest for the cat.
2. Dusting the cat with an insecticidal powder which is marked 'safe for cats'. This is the commonest approach to the problem. Most of these powders carry instructions telling you to brush the powder out of the coat after a certain period but others are safe to leave in the coat. Powders may either be dusted through the coat by hand or, by placing the cat in a pillow case with only its head sticking out, a quantity of powder can be shaken over the cat.

Cats with either ear mite infection, or any other ear infection, try to scratch in the area of the ear. Sometimes dirt from the hind-claws causes skin lesions in the area round the ears.

118

3. Spraying. Most sprays are particularly dangerous unless great care is taken to follow the instructions. They are effective since they often contain a more lethal form of insecticide which is safe for the cat when used sparingly. Some cats develop an allergic reaction to such sprays, although this is probably a reaction against the solvent rather than against the insecticide.

4. Flea collars. The original flea collars contained organophosphorus compounds and it was later proved that their continuous use could be harmful to the cat, although their use for a period of one or two weeks as treatment for a known flea infestation was quite safe. A collar containing a new insecticide has recently been marketed and this may prove useful.

Whichever treatment is used to remove the fleas from a cat, it must be supplemented by the cleansing of all bedding, baskets, etc. and the scattering of insecticidal powder into all obvious cracks and crevices.

Lice are fortunately less common than fleas. It would seem that healthy, clean cats are able to deal with lice themselves and heavy infestations only occur in young kittens and debilitated animals. Lice are grey or light brown in colour depending on whether they are of the sucking or biting variety, and for most of the time they remain stationary on the cat with their heads embedded in the skin. They cannot jump as fleas do, but move by crawling. The whole life cycle is spent on the cat, the female gluing her eggs on to the hair. The eggs are whitish specks which look like scurf and are known as nits.

Treatment is as for fleas (methods 1 or 2) and must be repeated at least once, after ten to fourteen days, in order to kill any newly hatched louse. Although lice cause skin irritation, the main problem is anaemia because a heavy infestation can drain a considerable quantity of blood from a kitten. In fact, even adult cats have been known to die from an untreated, heavy infestation of lice.

Notoedric and cheyletiella mites are all nearly microscopic and it is unlikely that you will be able to find any evidence of the actual mite's presence, other than an itchy cat with a thinning of the coat in the less furry regions such as the face (where notoedric mites occur) or tummy (where cheyletiella mites occur). An insecticidal treatment (methods 1 or 2) may prove successful but if not it is wise to obtain professional assistance from a vet in the microscopic identification of the mite.

Harvest mites are the same small mites which may crawl up your legs and bite you round the waist if you walk through stubble on an August day. On the cat they usually appear as small clusters of pinpoint-sized, orange or whitish dots. No treatment is necessary because they spend only a very short time on the mammalian host before dropping to the ground. If treatment is desired, however, methods 1 or 2 will rid the cat of the mites – until it next walks through a field!

Ticks are occasionally picked up from the grass by country cats, but the natural hosts of ticks are either sheep or birds. Some ticks look rather like brown or grey warts and have been mistaken by owners for growths or cysts. The sheep tick in particular buries its head and mouthparts very deeply in the skin and when attempts are made to remove the tick by pulling, these mouthparts frequently remain embedded and a swelling appears which persists for some time. It is advisable to either dope the tick with a spot of surgical spirit or alcohol, or to kill it with an insecticidal powder, before attempting to remove it.

Ear mites (otodectic mite infestation). If your cat produces a brown or blackish waxy material in its ear then it is one of a very great number which is infected with ear mites. The actual mite is white and only just visible to the naked eye. It lives in the outer ear among the waxy secretions which the ear produces in increased amounts as a reaction to the irritation. Strangely, many cats do not seem particularly worried by the presence of ear mites; perhaps they relieve the irritation by frequent washing, for let those same mites crawl on to your dog and there will be endless ear scratching.

Treatment must be aimed at applying an insecticide to the mites and not just to the outside wax. Many preparations can be obtained for the treatment of this condition, but all will fail unless you first clean the ears of excessive wax. This may be done with olive oil if the wax is hard, or with 1 percent cetrimide, followed by application of insecticidal powder or drops made specifically for the purpose. This is a condition where the owner sometimes has to resort to the vet due to lack of co-operation from the patient.

Treatment must be repeated at least twice a week for three weeks.

Ringworm is a condition which must be treated by a veterinary surgeon simply because it is highly infectious to the human race, particularly to children. It is also the most serious skin condition of the cat. Unfortunately it is unobtrusive and is frequently not recognized until some member of the family develops itchy areas on their own skin. Ringworm is not caused by a worm, nor by an insect but by a fungus and any dressing designed to kill the fungus will inevitably harm the cat. An effective treatment called griseofulvin is now available but the pills must be given for at least four weeks and often considerably longer. During this whole period any lesion on the cat is still infectious and you must harden your heart and confine the cat in an empty room or a rabbit hutch. All bedding used by the cat should be burned or disinfected by immersing it in a warm solution of 5 percent formaldehyde for at least twelve hours.

In some cases the cat may have obvious lesions which have a bare-skinned centre surrounded by an area of broken hairs which can be pulled out from the skin very easily. Your veterinary surgeon will probably advise you to remove and burn any of this loose hair and may also give you an ointment to apply to the area.

NURSING A CAT

Perhaps the most common disease of the cat is cat flu, a term which covers a number of virus conditions of varying virulence. Good nursing techniques are more essential for the treatment of cat flu than for any other cat disease, and the principles described here exemplify nursing in general. If you can nurse a cat through a really bad attack of cat flu, you should be able to nurse a cat through almost any ailment. Cat flu can occur in any age of cat but is most common in growing kittens. The first signs are usually conjunctivitis with the eyes partially closed, an increased flow of tears and the appearance of wetter-than-usual nostrils. Occasionally there is incessant sneezing and drooling from the mouth, giving the appearance of an acute hay fever attack, persisting for between twelve and twenty-four hours. In other cases gulping motions denoting a sore throat may be the first sign. The cat may still show a desire for food, coming forward when it is presented, but may only take a few mouthfuls. Prompt treatment by a veterinary surgeon at this early stage is most rewarding. The course of the illness is invariably cut short and your cat will probably make a quick recovery.

If these early signs are ignored, the discharge from the eyes may become purulent and conjunctival oedema may occur. There will be a purulent discharge from the nose so that the cat looks like a human with a severe head cold – and probably feels like one. It may also develop a temperature. Without sound nursing bronchitis – and later pneumonia – may develop, in which case the cat will either sit up with its neck held straight in order to obtain a freer passage of air at each breath or, when too exhausted, lie on its front fighting for breath. In many cases all food is refused for at least three weeks so the cat becomes emaciated and dies as much from general weakness as from the original disease.

Nursing should be considered as a supplement to veterinary treatment. Your veterinary surgeon will treat the condition with antibiotics in the form of injections or pills and will instruct you on how to use eye ointments for the treatment of conjunctivitis, how to give your cat a pill and how to clean and dress a cat's eye. These techniques are best learned first by example.

Good nursing is based on three essentials:
1. Maintenance of an even temperature.
2. Maintenance of body fluids.
3. Knowing your cat – the correct psychological approach.

There is no single, successful procedure in nursing and it is the interaction of effort involving these three essential factors that produces the results. The cat that insists on solitude must be nursed in a quiet 'hospital' corner away from other activities, and a large cardboard box with a piece of blanket in the bottom, in the corner of a little used room, is ideal. Heat is best provided by means of an infra-red heating lamp suspended over the box. The height at which the lamp should be suspended depends upon the warmth of the room; in general a height of about 5 feet (1·5 metres) is acceptable in summer, whilst about 3 feet (1 metre) may be better in winter. It must not provide so much heat that the cat feels uncomfortable and struggles to get away to find a cold spot, however. Another ideal 'hospital' is an

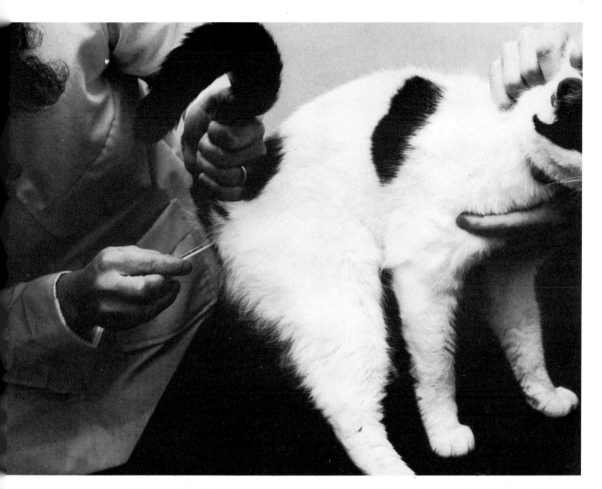

How to take a cat's rectal temperature. The normal temperature is 101·5°F (38·6°C), and temperatures in excess of 103°F (39·5°C) must be taken seriously.

airing cupboard, and many owners have nursed their sick cats back to health at the expense of unaired linen.

On the other hand, the cat that insists on human companionship must receive it and in these cases it is better to have the 'hospital' area in a much-used part of the house, preferably in a warm kitchen. Owners have been known to provide an even temperature for such companion-loving kittens by carrying them around inside their shirts and even taking them to bed. The aim in all cases is constant body warmth; it is no use providing a hot water bottle which at first is so hot that the cat moves away and later so cold that it is useless.

Perhaps the most serious side effect of cat flu is that in the majority of cases the patient refuses to eat or drink. The causes of this total refusal are various. In the early stages the throat may be sore and eating or even drinking is painful. Later, the nose may be blocked and it would seem that a cat is stimulated to eat more by its sense of

smell than by any other factor. Many cats refuse to accept food unless they can smell it. In addition to these factors it would seem that the cat flu viruses cause a depression somewhat similar to that caused by those of human flu, and the cat does not feel well enough to eat. This is particularly common in the oriental (Siamese and Burmese) breeds, which are prone to turn their faces to the wall and lose the will to live. The cat, originally a desert-living animal, can go without food for a considerable time – at least three weeks. Under normal circumstances cats can also survive without fluid for several days without coming to much harm, providing they remain inactive. The position is complicated in disease by the temperature factor, however, for when the body temperature is raised the fluid loss is greater. The maintenance of body fluids is therefore essential.

How do you tell if your cat is lacking fluid (dehydrated)? If you lift up some of the skin from the cat's back or chest with your thumb and forefinger, it should flow back into its normal position as soon as you let go. If the cat is dehydrated, however, the fold of skin will remain up in a ridge for several seconds.

The average cat requires about a cupful (225ml) of water daily, mainly in its solid food. Of this cupful about half is lost in urine and the remainder is circulated, used and lost both through breathing and in the production of faeces. When a cat is not eating, these losses in urine and respiration do not necessarily diminish and therefore you should try and ensure that your cat still receives approximately a cupful of fluid daily. The most beneficial fluids are water, normal saline (1 teaspoon of salt in a pint of water or 2 teaspoons of salt in a litre of water), glucose water, glucose saline (1 dessertspoon of glucose powder in a pint of water or 2 dessertspoons of glucose powder in a litre of water), milk, solutions of beef or yeast extract, tea and fruit drinks, depending on which your cat finds most acceptable. If you can persuade your cat to swallow liquids, the additional salts or sugars are beneficial but the essential element is the water. The attention-loving cat may be persuaded to lap a little from a spoon or, failing this, allow you to dribble fluid from a spoon into the side of its mouth. There is no need to give much at a time, a teaspoonful or two every hour is sufficient. Alternatively, many cats will swallow liquid if it is squirted very gently between their teeth by means of a small, plastic syringe, although for cats that try to chew the nozzle it is wise to protect it with a small piece of rubber tubing to prevent splintering. Some cats will best take liquids in the form of smashed ice cubes, which may be dropped on to the back of the tongue. These cubes may be of plain ice or iced glucose water, etc. Feeding the solitary cat is much more difficult, for many of these resist all attempts to take liquids in any form into their mouths. You might try wrapping such a cat in a warm towel so that it cannot get its legs free and then try to get some liquid into its mouth from a syringe; but if the cat still struggles leave it alone for it will lose more strength (and fluid) in its struggling effort than you will be able to replace. Such totally unco-operative patients can only be fed fluids successfully by means of saline drips. These must be given initially by a veterinary surgeon and entail injecting the fluid under the skin once

or twice daily until the balance is restored.

The cat's comfort is important and discharges from the eyes, nose and mouth should be removed frequently. This may be done with damp cottonwool or, if the discharge is hard, with cottonwool soaked in water, saline or a very weak disinfectant such as 1 percent cetrimide. An antibiotic eye ointment placed in the conjunctival sac, at least three times a day, will help to clear the eye. Again, of course, not all cats will tolerate such attentions and you have to balance the value of the treatment against the disturbance of the cat. It is particularly useful to clear the nostrils of mucus whenever possible and some cats will tolerate inhalations of menthol or friar's balsam. Obviously no cat will tolerate the towel-over-the-head method as used for children but various techniques can be tried. One particular Persian chose her own 'hospital' area – a chair seat under the dining room table – and her owner, finding that menthol and friar's balsam inhalations helped her breathing, set up a kettle on top of a small oil stove under the table and draped blankets over the edge. If you should try some similar makeshift method do beware of the fire risk!

Unfortunately the lack of sense of smell, although partially due to a blocked nose, may also be due to swelling of the tissues or possibly even to a direct effect on the nerve endings, so even after the nose is apparently clear the cat may still have little sense of smell. It is at this point that you should offer the most strongly smelling piece of fish that can be found, or a particularly ripe bit of cheese, for if the cat can be persuaded to take even a few morsels of some seemingly unsuitable food the battle is won. Foods such as prawns, shellfish and scampi have all proved successful starters at some time. Once the cat starts to eat, you can feed all the most nutritious foods available – chicken, liver, food concentrates or just ordinary tinned cat foods – but to start it eating you need something highly odorous.

It is as well to remember that cats which have refused food for considerable periods will suffer from a deficiency of certain essential vitamins, the most important of which are vitamin A and vitamin B_{12}. Your veterinary surgeon may remedy this by an injection, but even so it is advisable to offer foods rich in vitamin A during the convalescent period. Such foods include fresh

butter, beef fat, cream cheese, fish oils, liver and fish roes. (Many of these are also rich in B_{12}.)

Sometimes all your efforts seem of no avail and your cat, particularly if it is a Siamese, just lies there refusing to take an interest in life. In such cats quiet, personal contact sometimes helps. Just holding, stroking and talking to the cat, or sometimes just lifting it up and carrying it out into the garden to have a brief look at the sunshine and the birds may be enough to perk it up. Never give up, and never give way to anger at the cat's apparent determination to die, for if at this stage you try to force feed the animal, it will die in the struggle.

Sometimes it is neither your veterinary surgeon nor you who win the battle, but another cat. There is no doubt that the most comforting sensation that a cat can appreciate is a good wash, and occasionally another cat will lick a companion back to life. This raises the question of isolation to prevent the spread of an infectious disease. Many of you will have a single cat but even for a household with two or three cats it is probably not worth trying to prevent the

spread of the infection but better to rely on catching the symptoms early and so curtailing the disease. The only way to prevent the spread of a highly infectious disease is by strict isolation, which involves the nurse wearing protective clothing which is changed after every visit to the patient. Even so the infection may still spread, as many cases, even when apparently fully recovered, remain carriers of the disease for considerable periods.

To nurse your cat back to health in such a way may sound laborious but many people tell of the wonderful reward the cat gives in the form of increased affection. After treating undemonstrative cats – cats that hitherto would never sit on laps or even like to be stroked – they often become the most affectionate, grateful and home-loving animals. A really satisfying reward for the effort put into nursing your cat.

KITTENING

Most queens can manage to produce a litter of kittens without human interference, but those that do get into difficulties may require a special form of attention, and as midwifery is all part of nursing this is discussed here.

If a queen is having difficulty she may give up trying to pass a kitten through the birth canal when only half the kitten is exposed. This is one of the few times when the owner may save a kitten's life without endangering that of the queen. As a midwife you must be as clean as possible and you should have an assistant. Wash your hands thoroughly while your assistant fetches a clean towel and then assists by holding the queen firmly but gently round the shoulders. Examine the emerging kitten. You must look for either the head and one or two forelegs, or for the tail and hindlegs. If you see either of these combinations grasp as much of the kitten as possible through a single thickness of the towel and pull very gently. If this does not work, try to readjust the kitten's position in the pelvis by pushing it back into the pelvis about $\frac{1}{2}$ inch (1 cm) and then turning it slightly. *Gentle* side-to-side traction is of far more assistance in aiding delivery than a straight pull. Should gentle assistance fail, a veterinary surgeon should be contacted immediately. He will almost certainly be too late to save that kitten, but other kittens may still be saved.

Another common problem is that of the kitten that does not start to breathe spontaneously. This may be caused by a number of reasons, the most common being that the queen is tired and has not finished her task. In other words, she has produced the kitten but she has not cleaned away the membranes or given the kitten a stimulating wash and the kitten lies in its sac making vain attempts to draw air into its lungs. Grasp the membranes with a dry towel and peel them off the face and head and wipe the mouth and nose and see that there is no fluid in the mouth. If the kitten is still wet a vigorous rub over the whole body will help to stimulate respiration, often causing screams of apparent indignation, screams which efficiently open up the lungs.

The umbilical cord connecting the kitten to the placenta is normally severed by the queen herself. Should it still be intact it may be torn. Many textbooks, instructional books and breeders' guides give a list of instruments and materials which they say are absolutely essential for dealing with the umbilical cord. In fact, instruments are not necessary. In nature the cord is best severed by the mother biting it, and even if she neglects to do this it will soon break naturally for it has this inherent tendency. Many umbilical hernias have been caused by human interference. Of course, if your hands are really clean and scrubbed, and you know how to tear an umbilical cord without producing a hernia, then go ahead – but, if you have any doubts leave it to nature. Do not attempt to use ligatures and scissors.

Each kitten has its own placenta and foetal membranes, and it is normal and right that the mother should chew and swallow as many of them as she likes, however unpleasant it seems to you.

Post-partum haemorrhage (bleeding after giving birth)

There is always a small amount of blood passed after kittening but if this should be excessive the cat will become weak and her tongue will be obviously pale. These are signs of serious haemorrhage and veterinary assistance should be sought without delay. Most cats recover from kittening difficulties very rapidly but if inflammation of the womb should develop (metritis), you will see (or smell) a thickish, brown discharge from the vulva. The queen will be off her food, uncomfortable, thirsty, and will probably have lost interest in her kittens. Again, call your veterinary surgeon or you will lose not only the queen but also her kittens.

Perhaps the subject of kittening should not be dismissed so shortly for it is a fascinating theme. Queens have their chosen 'laying in' areas; some confide in their owners asking that a certain cupboard door should be opened while others, seeming to sense that their kittens are unwanted, disappear to kitten down in a distant hiding place. Between these two extremes are those that have as their favourite delivery area your best eiderdown, or still others that call their owners to be near to watch this wonder of nature. This is not the place to discuss the joys of parenthood but cat lovers will delight you with tales of carrying and kitten hiding, kitten sitters, kitten training and the instinctive nursing by toms and neuters when the necessity arises.

It is hoped that you will have many years of joy, comfort, communication and affection from your cats and that these aids to home nursing need only rarely be used.

Cats and the law

The following is intended to do no more than provide the reader with a basic and elementary understanding of the law as it affects cats. It should not be used as a basis for litigation without first consulting a solicitor.

Cats as objects of theft All animals which have a tangible value and belong to someone can be the object of theft. Anyone who picks up a well-fed cat in the street and takes it home with intent to deprive its owner permanently of its possession is guilty, prima facie, of the offence of theft. (Theft Act 1968.) It may be argued, however, that the accused person honestly believed that the cat was a stray. Alternatively, the defence may be offered that the intention was merely to take the cat home to feed it, with a view to setting it free thereafter. But few magistrates or judges will believe that a well-cared-for cat with an expensive collar around its neck was thought to be a stray, or that an expensive variety of cat belonged to that category. Equally, anyone picking up another person's cat and taking it home for a week could hardly confidently argue that his intention was merely to give it a good feed before releasing it. Just as it is an offence to steal a cat so it is also an offence to receive a cat knowing it to be stolen or believing it to have been stolen.

Trespass by a cat The laws of trespass do not apply to domestic animals such as cats and dogs although the latter may be destroyed and the owner fined if the worrying of domestic stock takes place. For obvious reasons this does not apply to cats or to their owners and, in this respect, the law holds that a person wishing to prevent the entry of cats upon his property must provide a wall or fence to keep them out. Even if your cat walks into a garden and digs up the owner's favourite bulbs you cannot be held liable. A person finding a cat upon his land has a right to eject it (he must not, in fact, retain it), but he must do so without the use of unnecessary force. He may also request that the owner remove the cat. Should he throw something at the cat so as to hurt or kill it, he is committing an offence and the owner may sue him for damage. He may also be punished for causing the cat unnecessary suffering. Furthermore, he must not threaten the owner of the cat. Conversely, a cat owner who deliberately puts his cat over a neighbour's wall in order to cause annoyance or to do damage to his neighbour's property is himself guilty of an offence, for the law holds that a person must so use his property so as not to damage that of another.

Cruelty to cats The law protects all living creatures, including the cat, against cruelty, but just what is required to constitute cruelty is for the courts to decide. The word 'cruelty' in its legal context is not limited to actual bodily harm. It would be cruel, for example, to imprison a cat in a tiny space for an unreasonable period of time. Similarly, it would be considered cruelty to starve a cat to the degree that it exhibited signs of marked emaciation. In general, the degree of cruelty sufficient to break the law would be measured by whether or not such treatment would seem abhorrent to the average, decent person.

Cats and medical research Such terms as 'vivisection' carry a highly emotive implication. In Britain the use of animals for research is strictly controlled by the Home Office which issues licences to highly reputable medical research laboratories and carries out inspection of all premises so licensed. In Britain the bulk of animal experiments consist of nothing more than the use of animals for standardizing the doses of drugs. Such experiments are neither painful nor dangerous, and the animals so used are well cared for. Nevertheless, many experiments are undoubtedly carried out which involve surgery of varying degrees of complexity, and it cannot be reasonably denied that from these experiments a great deal of benefit accrues, both to man and to animals in general. Laws lay down that no painful surgery may be inflicted without anaesthetic and if the nature of the surgery is such that on awaking the animal is likely to feel severe or prolonged pain, it must not be allowed to regain consciousness. It is hoped that the advent of tissue culture techniques, together with the growth of a greater spirit of compassion in man, will progressively reduce the number of experiments performed upon animals.

The laws governing the sale of cats Under the Trade Descriptions Act it is the seller's duty to ensure that any advertising or similar inducement he displays gives a just and proper description of the goods or services offered for sale and that such advertisements are not in any way misleading. Where a shop or breeder sells a pedigree animal it is now very important to ensure that its description is absolutely factual. A pedigree cat may be defined as being one in respect of which the seller issues a certification showing the parents, grandparents and great-grandparents. Anyone may issue a pedigree, but such a document is of virtually no value unless it is issued and certified by the Governing Council of the Cat Fancy. Where the kitten has not, as yet, been registered the pedigree and registration certificates of both parents should be examined and, in either case, you should not part with any money until you have received a signed Governing Council of the Cat Fancy Transfer Certificate. Under no circumstances should the buyer of a pedigree kitten accept any special conditions of sale, such as, for example, that the breeder has the right to the pick of the first or subsequent litters born to the cat which they are selling. Such conditions are not illegal, but the Cat Fancy frowns upon them.

Kittens dying soon after sale It is the duty of the seller to ensure that the kitten sold to a buyer is in good health, but the buyer is expected to use reasonable common sense in deciding this fact for himself. A kitten which falls ill and perhaps even dies soon after changing hands may have contracted the illness before the sale, or may have contracted it afterwards. The buyer would only have a case against the seller where he could prove that the latter knew the kitten was ill. This is generally almost impossible to establish unless the buyer can prove that the seller had an illness on his premises at the time of the sale. If you have grounds for believing that you have been sold a sick kitten or a kitten which was incorrectly described by a breeder who is a member of the Cat Fancy, you should send the relevant information to the Secretary:
Mrs. W. Davis
Dovefields,
Petworth Road,
Witley, Surrey

Exporting kittens If you acquire a female pedigree cat you may decide to breed with her, and may subsequently find that you have more kittens than you wish to keep. It is your responsibility as the breeder to try and ensure that any kittens you sell go to good homes. Occasionally, foreign breeders may answer your advertisements, and novice breeders should be warned that the standards and conditions for cats to which we are accustomed in Britain are not always as high in other countries. Therefore, treat enquiries from abroad for kittens or litters with great caution and only allow your kittens to be exported when you have personal knowledge of the would-be buyer or have obtained adequate assurances from a mutual friend.

The Feline Advisory Bureau No book about cats would be complete without reference to an organization which has done much to increase our knowledge of the cat from the veterinary point of view and to make such knowledge more freely available. It is probably best known to the public as a source of free and confidential advice on all aspects of cat owning, and particularly on the various diseases and conditions which affect cats. The Bureau maintains an advisory panel of experienced veterinary surgeons, scientists and doctors whose combined knowledge covers virtually every subject on which advice may be sought, and a comprehensive list of informative leaflets is available. A further function of the Bureau is to improve the standard of boarding catteries and, to this end, an inspection and approval scheme has been organized and is also available to cat owners. For those seeking assistance from the Feline Advisory Bureau or wishing to contribute financially to its aims, the name and address of its Hon. Secretary are:
Michael A. Findlay, B.V.M.S., M.R.C.V.S.
The Feline Advisory Bureau,
6, Woodthorpe Road,
Putney, London, SW15 6UQ.

Index